THE BEST IN

CONTEMPORARY

JEWELLERY

THE BEST IN

CONTEMPORARY

JEWELLERY

DAVID WATKINS

ROTOVISION

A QUARTO BOOK

Published by ROTOVISION SA
Route Suisse 9
CH-1295 Mies
Switzerland

Distributed to the trade in the United States by
Watson-Guptill Publications
1515 Broadway
New York, NY 10036

ISBN 0-8230-6361-5

This book was designed and produced by
Quarto Publishing plc
6 Blundell Street
London N7 9BH

Creative Director: Richard Dewing
Designer: Steve Miller
Project Editor: Stefanie Foster
Picture Researcher: Michele Faram
Editorial Assistant: Anna Briffa

Typeset in Great Britain by
Central Southern Typesetters, Eastbourne
Manufactured in Hong Kong by Regent Publishing Services Limited
Printed in China

Contents

Introduction   6

Idea   8

Object   26

Image   182

Artist Profiles   208

Index   222

Photographic Credits   224

Introduction

Contemporary jewellery, as a more-or-less identifiable category, began with isolated individuals and in isolated national and regional centres through the 1950s and 1960s, emerging as an international movement in the early 1970s. Its early development was dependent on the activities of a small number of artists and their supporters around the world. It has always projected a strong sense of individualism, standing out for innovation and aesthetics rather than for commercialism.

Contemporary jewellery now exists within a well-established international network of shared knowledge and experience, of interrelated but often disputing philosophies. Its base has increased not only in terms of the sheer number of artists, but also the amount and level of academic provision, the number of galleries, of museum and scholarly exhibitions, and the distribution of international centres of significant activity.

This book presents a snapshot of current international contemporary jewellery. It inevitably reflects a particular view. The response of artists in submitting work for inclusion has been extraordinarily positive, so that this selection is, within its own terms, as near comprehensive as could have been hoped for. It does not, on the other hand, include experiments or appropriations by artists operating at the periphery, where the definition of jewellery merges with or becomes subsumed within clothing art or performance art, for instance, but concentrates on the distinguishing core activity of jewellery.

This last discrimination aside, there has been no intention to discriminate positively or negatively in terms of materials used, processes, philosophy, age, gender or nationality; but selection has been guided by the criteria of authentic originality and coherence of vision, and these criteria have been given greater priority than outright novelty.

Fourteen countries are represented. Of these, Germany achieves a 25 per cent share — twice that of its nearest rivals, The Netherlands and the USA, and about three times that of Italy and Great Britain. It is not the purpose of this book to explore the reasons for such a balance, but it must relate primarily to inherent opportunities in the embedded culture of each country.

In all, 64 artists are presented, their ages ranging from 30 to 74 years, with an average of 47. One third are women — probably a high proportion compared with established professionals in the plastic arts generally — and their average age is five years younger than that of the men. One possible interpretation of this is that the gender balance of a future selection would shift further towards the women.

At least half of the artists regularly teach or have taught their subject at some time, seventeen of them at the level of professor. However this is interpreted, the establishment of contemporary jewellery studies within universities and colleges around the world seems unarguable, and increasing numbers of young artists seeking places in schools over the past decade confirm the increasingly broad appeal of the subject.

The organisation of the book into the three sections, Idea, Object and Image – corresponding to a "portfolio" of sketch designs, a "gallery show" of pieces, and a "live show" – sets out to give a taste of the conceptual context within which artists work, but its main focus is a celebration of the work itself and especially the individual achievements of this growing international community of contemporary jewellers.

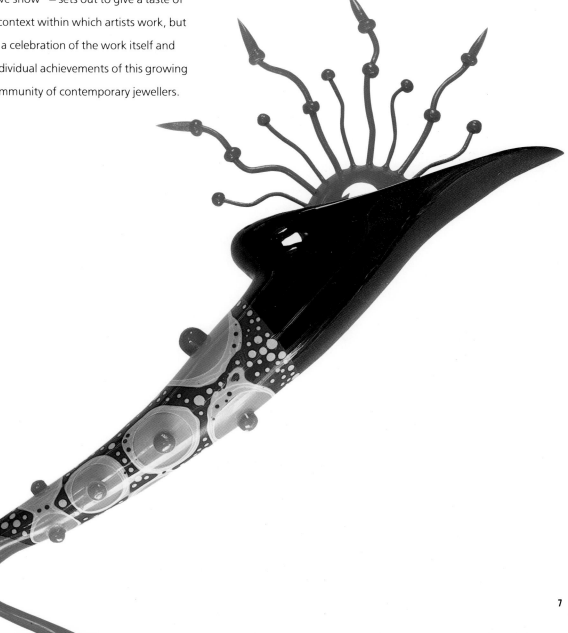

IDEA

Some elements of practice and craft knowledge are necessarily common to most contemporary jewellers, but when it comes to the visual development and graphic representation of ideas or designs for individual pieces, there are now — outside the world of commercial practice — no conventions, no consensus and no objective standards. Many artist-jewellers, including those who have been classically trained in such skills, would regard them as at best redundant, at worst an impediment to the real experience of discovering and communicating through process and object and, inevitably, irreconcilable with their own individualism. Most will, however, keep sketch books, models or trial pieces, and these will remain essentially private.

The selection of contributions included in this section aims, through a small number of drawings and models which were not strictly speaking intended for publication, to give some indication of the way ideas arise, and are tested or recorded. The majority of artists chose not to offer examples, which is in itself revealing. Of course, many jewellers or goldsmiths, while extraordinarily skilful in their own very difficult craft, have found it less necessary to develop their graphic skills, regarding them as of little importance. Only a few view them as an important element of their conceptual and working routine. All are also by nature perfectionists. Even so, this element, precisely because it is not subject to convention, is usually informative and expressive.

Making jewellery can be a slow and troublesome business: the period for the gestation of ideas, consequently long, and typically bound up with the physical phenomena and attributes of materials and processes. "Design development", if one may call it such, may take many turns, but there is no compelling reason why it should even exist in a tangible or communicable sense, unless required by a commissioning client. Since the over-riding priority of the jewellers in this book is to follow ideas and create objects for their own sake rather than for a specific client, even this requirement is comparatively rare. It should be said, of course, that it is this very independence of spirit that excites and sustains kindred clients and collectors.

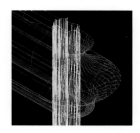

Some artists find a particular technique of drawing or modelling appropriate to the rhythm or style of their work, and rarely diverge from it. One can probably guess the examples here to which this would apply. Others use different means at different times, or according to changing factors — such as the scale, processes, materials or preoccupations of their jewellery at the time. Many will combine a number of conceptual and practical techniques, to examine different aspects of the same idea. An interesting and challenging subset, reveals how thoughts about jewellery may be set within much broader, or layered, conceptual frameworks — of philosophy, culture, physical space — than might be anticipated, engaging in "larger" concerns, or a sort of conceptual limbering-up.

Amongst the attractions of making jewellery in the way most of these artists do — carrying out the whole physical process from inception to completion — is that intuition and the senses are active, processing and contributing throughout the whole endeavour. It is, of course, possible to develop and test an idea quite exhaustively, whether on paper or through models, before beginning to make the piece. Some do, and it may be very helpful, for example, when a procedure is likely to be very complicated or require great precision. Computer Aided Design (CAD/CAM) is very interesting in this respect but, while offering its own dimensional and conceptual benefits, it cannot, however, overcome its inability to involve the full range of physical sensibilities. Most artist-jewellers would probably regard these as critical and indivisible elements in the generation and development of ideas as well as objects. From this point of view, developing an idea too highly at the outset could compromise immediacy at every other stage. This is not the whole story, but it seems to be a strong theme.

Giampaolo Babetto

One can often find correlations between jewellery and architecture – something about the issues of structure and ornament, perhaps – but rarely on such a direct level or to such sensual ends. Babetto once began to train to be an architect.

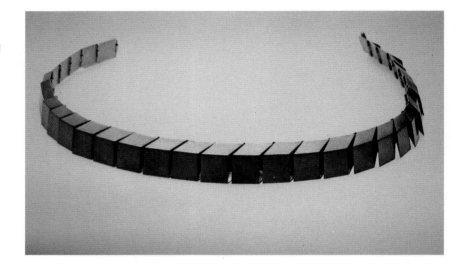

Inspiration for a necklace

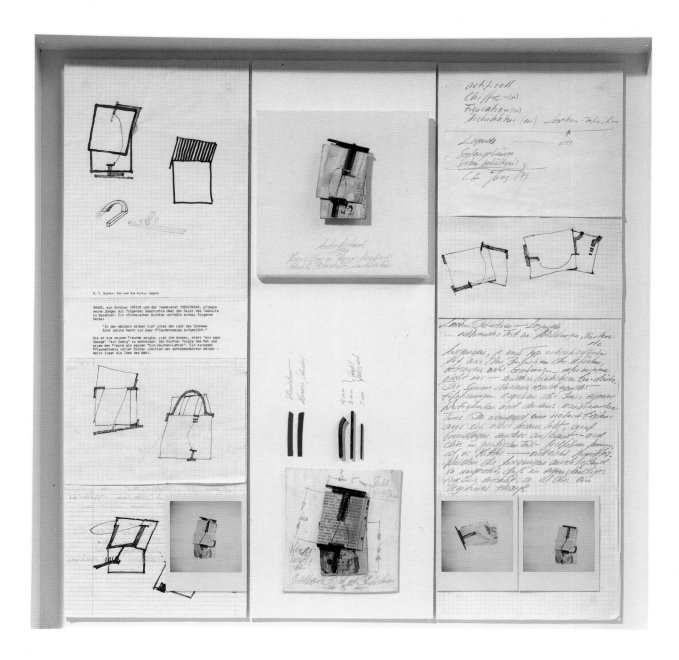

Rudiger Lorenzen

Lorenzen offers a view of inspiration, introspection and
synthesis – some components of the creative process. It is
possible for a piece of jewellery to carry a considerable
meaning.

Drawings, text and photographs in connection with *Legende
No. 9* 1992

Anton Cepka

Cepka's sketches are light and insubstantial, indicating the
skeletons of installations or provisional architecture. The
playing out of grand schemes on a miniature scale is a
recurring theme in jewellery, as is the evident enjoyment
of repetition Cepka displays.

Sketches for brooches 1993

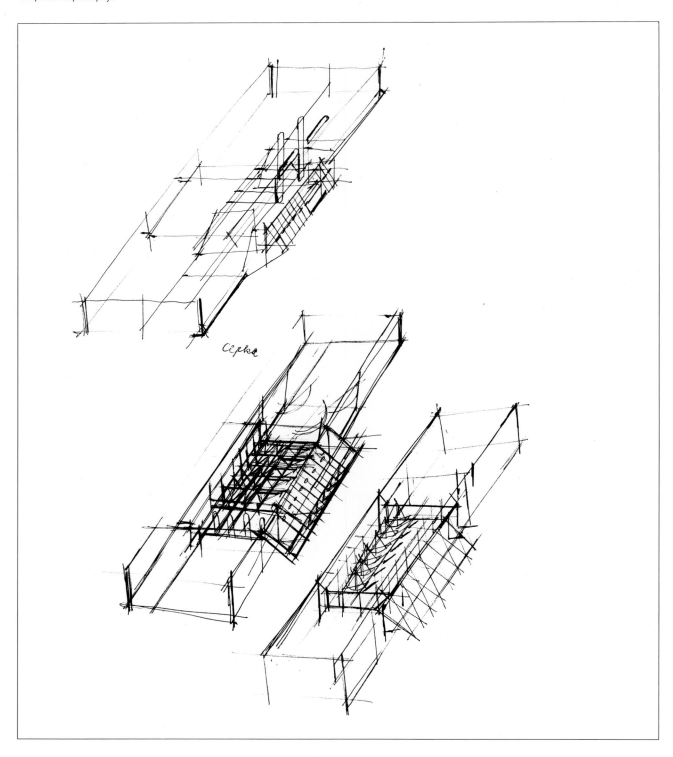

Wolfgang Rahs

A sculpture applied to a smelting furnace which is, at the same time, a model exploring the idea of "case".

Case on Radwerk / Kiste am Radwerk 1990

This sculpture, based on an ancient Scythian travelling table, provides a real insight into Rahs' poetic intentions and actions. It combines a study and work table within a travel case – "for the planned departure over the iron routes, into the Caucasian region."

Case at Graz Main Station / Kiste am Hauptbahnhof Graz 1990

Onno Boekhoudt

Boekhoudt's eye for the affinities between jewellery and sculpture is clearly evident, and this work illustrates how a jeweller will habitually think at different scales in order to explore an idea. The models are indeed an exploration of pure form but, in their respect for material, their sensitivity to nuance, and their simple dignity, they also foreshadow the craft that will follow.

Models for rings in painted wood 1991

William Harper

This drawing is not related to any specific piece of
jewellery – Harper describes it as "adjunct" – but its
undisguised message is that the core subject matter of his
jewellery is himself.

Drawing / collage: *Self-portrait of the Artist . . . Possessed* 1992

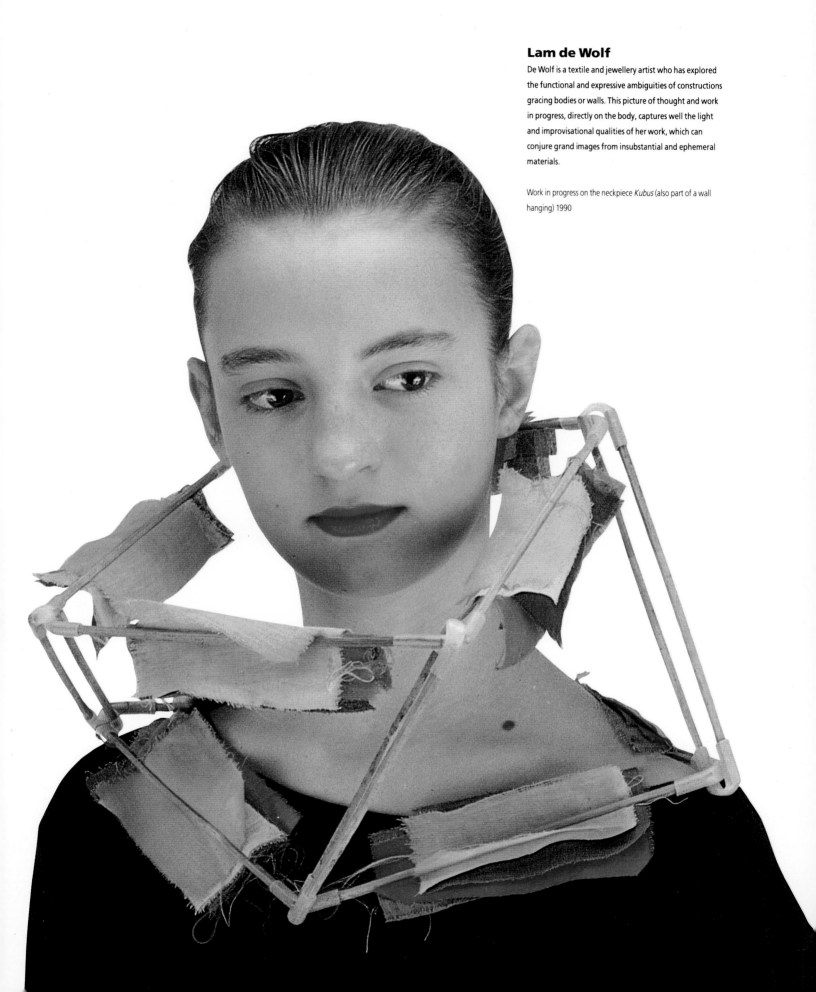

Lam de Wolf

De Wolf is a textile and jewellery artist who has explored the functional and expressive ambiguities of constructions gracing bodies or walls. This picture of thought and work in progress, directly on the body, captures well the light and improvisational qualities of her work, which can conjure grand images from insubstantial and ephemeral materials.

Work in progress on the neckpiece *Kubus* (also part of a wall hanging) 1990

Wilhelm Mattar

A literal and – although the effect is ironically undermined – still horrifying figurative model by Mattar. A three-dimensional equivalent of a thumb-nail sketch with the kind of immediacy that would suggest.

Model for a brooch

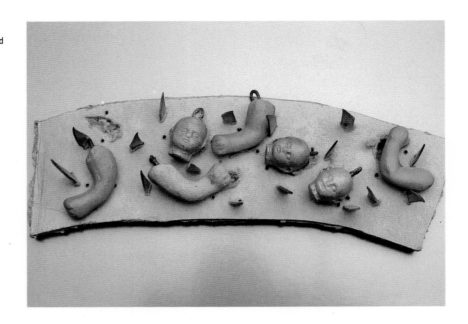

Fritz Maierhofer

For Maierhofer, a model is a stage in a rational process of developing or evaluating an idea. It need not be too precise in itself but, before beginning to make the real thing, he must first understand its form and decide precisely how it must be constructed.

Models for three brooches 1991

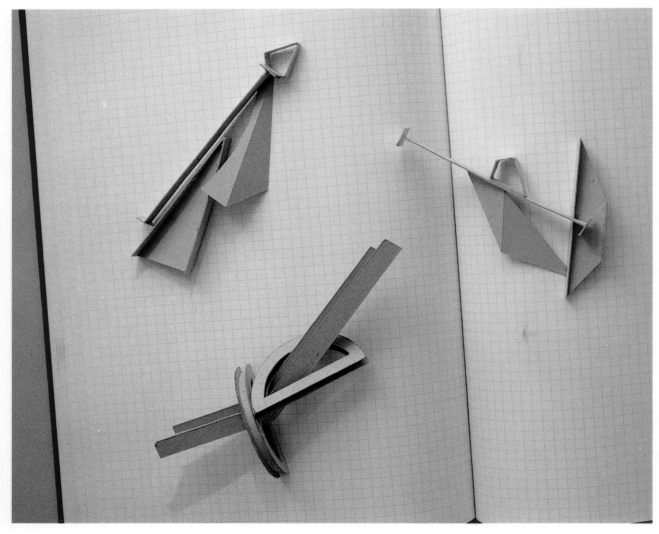

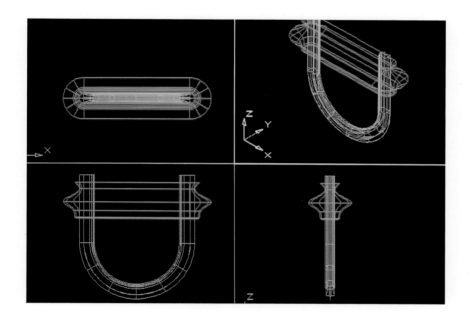

Stanley Lechtzin

Computers now offer any artist the opportunity to make non-physical models. The process is not necessarily quicker, and it must sacrifice the physical interaction with material which many jewellers would regard as essential to their creativity, but for some the challenge to traditional practice is necessary if not irresistible.

CAD Wire frame models for the bracelet *Archbrace #38F* 1992

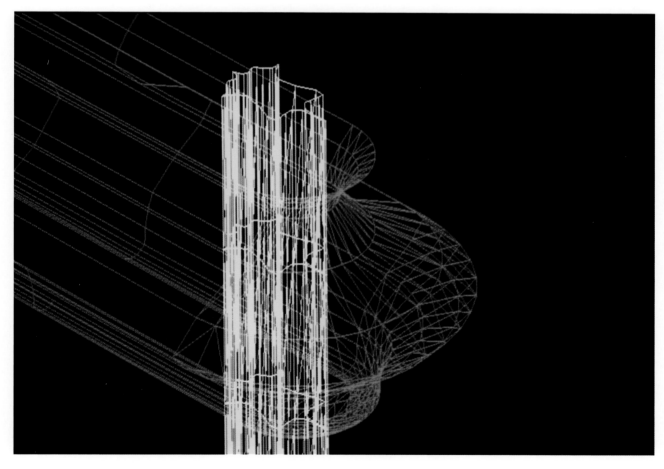

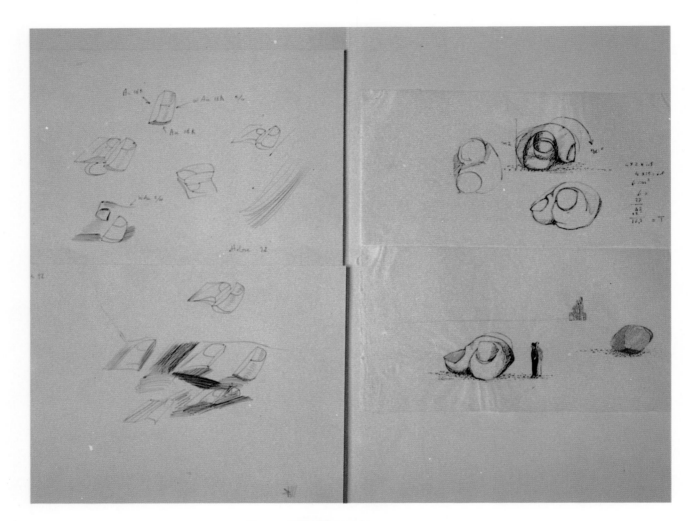

Bruno Martinazzi

Martinazzi moves easily between miniature and
monumental scales in his sketch book, and the interplay
persists in his works. He is also a sculptor. His jewellery,
although small, can seem monumental, and his sculpture
usually is.

Drawing for the ring *Dike* 1992

Philip Sajet

Impressionistic, certainly, but also impatient and unprecious. Sajet's painting carries some (perhaps intended) irony. After all, for a jeweller, attention to detail and patience are virtually a *priori*. Some well-known jewellery designers have made ambiguous sketches, passing them on to craftsmen for final realisation. Such a contingency would not even occur to Sajet.

Painting (sketch) for the neckpiece *Thunder and Lightning* 1993

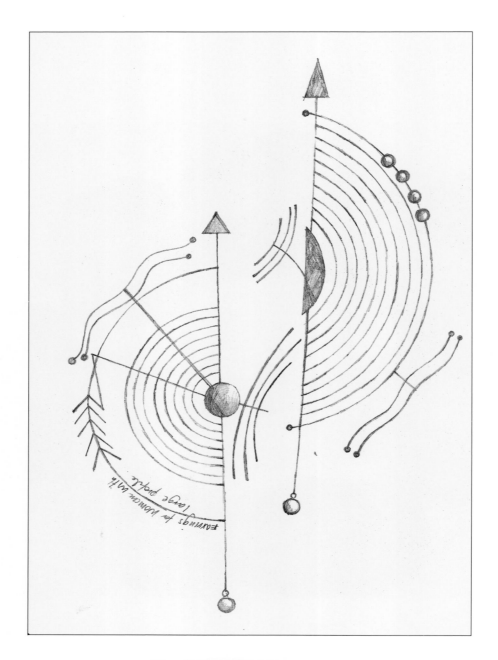

Wendy Ramshaw

Ramshaw's drawing is typically compositional and diagrammatic – like a map, with little indication of substance – but improvisational, enjoying the intricacies of geometry in motion. Her drawings are made quickly and in profusion, serving first as *aides memoires,* but, since they are of the size of a piece of jewellery, they can also function as working templates.

Drawing for *Earrings for Woman with Large Profile* 1989

Hermann Jünger

Jünger's graphic explorations of jewellery themes are
notable on many levels, not least for their close
correspondence with his approach to making. The
drawings, too, become artefacts which are dense in
texture, surface, weight and gesture.

A page of sketches 1992

Susan Cohn

For some jewellers, or some types of jewellery problem, it is necessary to think with the fingers, in which case methods are likely to be quick and simple. Although it can be difficult to sustain a sense of such spontaneity through the more laborious stages of making, it is often an essential element of the idea or ideology.

Models for the series . . . *and does it work?* 1990

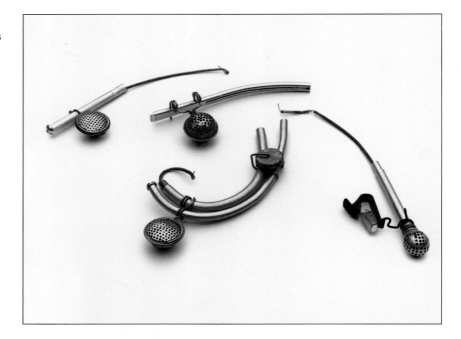

Models for the series *Cosmetic Manipulations* 1992

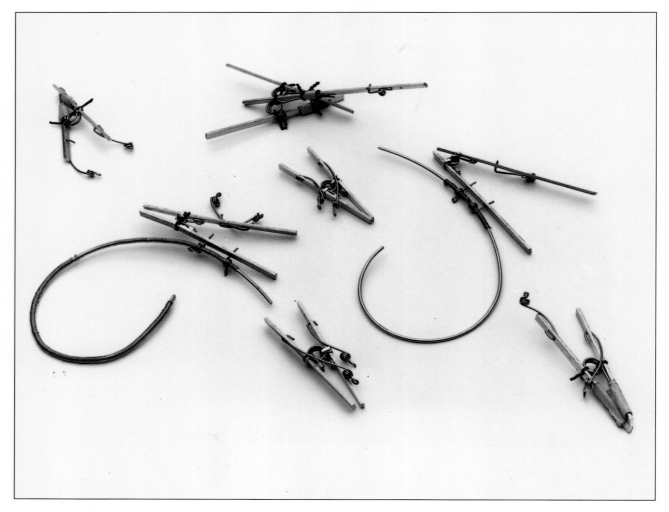

David Watkins

These drawings explore some generic characteristics of computer-aided modelling, which can throw up very singular forms and images – in this case, fragmented presences of indeterminate but possibly tremendous size. The "problem" is to find a way to realise them off-screen in such a way that some record of this impression persists.

Printed screen dumps of CAD models for brooches 1989

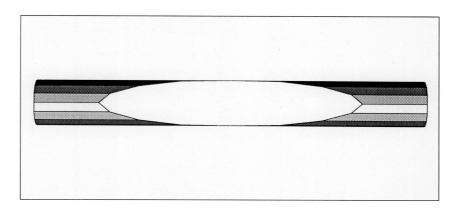

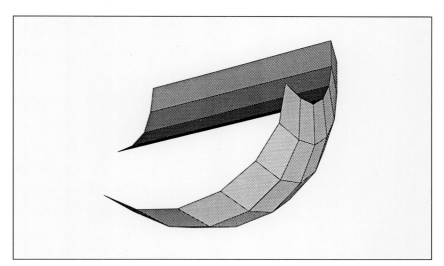

OBJECT

The jewellery is simply presented in this section, to be seen as it might be in a gallery or in the artist's studio. It is generally quite dissociated from any context or place, use or adornment, so that we may concentrate upon it as object.

Although this approach is a well-established convention, it is worth considering. To pursue the analogy of the gallery, which is where most of the work in this book will be seen, painting, sculpture and ceramics, for instance, will all inhabit the space in a way which is comfortably consistent with their basic physical relation to the real world — on the wall, floor, plinth or table. Jewellery is, despite its always ambiguous status, in a sense de-natured, and whatever its claims to merit as artefact, must, in this "free-standing" environment, operate at a disadvantage.

The fact is, however, that it competes well in this context. Over comparatively few years, contemporary jewellers have developed an innovative, challenging and absorbing field of activity that has extended far beyond any reasonable expectation, and with an energy which other applied arts, in particular, have found difficult to match. In a way, it has revealed a large subject in small objects. It has also developed to some extent to meet the very opportunities and demands of the situation described.

One consistent theme of contemporary jewellery is that it should be judged in its own terms as object, in much the same way as a piece of sculpture might be. That is not to say that the two are the same — although some would suggest that they are — but the aesthetic range of jewellery has nevertheless expanded beyond recognition. As one would expect in such circumstances, much of the work turns in on itself as a subject, testing its own assumptions, purposes, appropriate forms and meanings; some artists habitually refer to their work as "research" or "experiment".

But not all contemporary jewellers follow along these lines. For some, in evocation of an older tradition, the sense of service to others defines the whole activity. They will set a high value on direct interaction with collectors and clients, placing their skills at the disposal of those who need and appreciate them — a human transaction in which the jewellery becomes an agent of mediation and communication.

In this section, contemporary jewellers show many shades of interpretation as to the appropriate materials, subject matter, meanings and purposes of their art.

Giampaolo Babetto

Italy b. 1947

Babetto's early work was characterized by seductively
delicate chains of gold. In his later work, thin, hard sheets
of the noble metal are beaten out and scratched, invoking
its strong beauty and resilient values. Superficial
preciousness is not an issue. This outstanding goldsmith
combines archaic resonances with an authentically modern
voice.

Brooch 1992
18ct gold, pigment
6 x 6 x 0.6cm
Private collection

Neckpiece 1992
18ct gold, niello
75 x 0.5 x 0.5 cm
Private collection

Bracelet 1991
18ct gold, pigment
6 x 6 x 6cm
Private collection

Brooch 1992
18ct gold, pigment
6 x 6 x 0.6cm
Private collection

Ulrike Bahrs

Germany b.1944

Bahrs has used a wide range of the traditional materials and processes of the goldsmith. Her work has not been limited by a narrow aesthetic, but has kept contact with many periods and styles of jewellery, from primitive, through Romanesque, to Modern, and has remained very personal. This work is charged with the sensual pleasures of wearing jewellery.

4 Levels Reflect into the Sun
Neckpiece 1991
Gold, silver, crystal glass, hologram
Pendant: 6 × 9cm
Artist's collection

Egg, Wool and Metal
Necklace and bracelet 1990
Private collection

Gijs Bakker

The Netherlands b.1942

Bakker has been a very influential, and indispensable
contributor to the dialectics of contemporary jewellery in
Europe. His aesthetic is essentially that of a designer –
questioning, clarifying, formulating – and indeed he has
worked across a number of design disciplines. In his
jewellery, his acute insights and witty observations are
delivered with a combination of shrewd provocation and
disarmingly confident, but always impeccable,
presentation.

Adam
Collar 1988
PVC laminated photograph, gold-plated brass
Stedelijk Museum, Amsterdam / Royal College of Art, London /
National Museum of Modern Art, Kyoto

Nesty
Brooch 1991
PVC laminated photograph, white gold, diamonds
Artist's collection

Face
Brooch 1991
PVC laminated photograph, brilliant and baguette diamonds,
white gold
Marijke Vallanzasca, Padua, Italy

James Bennett

USA b.1948

Bennett uses enamel unconventionally, suppressing its naturally glassy surface and depth in favour of something more painterly, which gives the material a broad range of expression. These objects flicker between artefact and amulet but (primitively) ornamented with gold, they are drawn into the territory of jewellery. They are hollow, being built up by electroforming, a process which can also contribute its own "accidents" and nuances of form and texture.

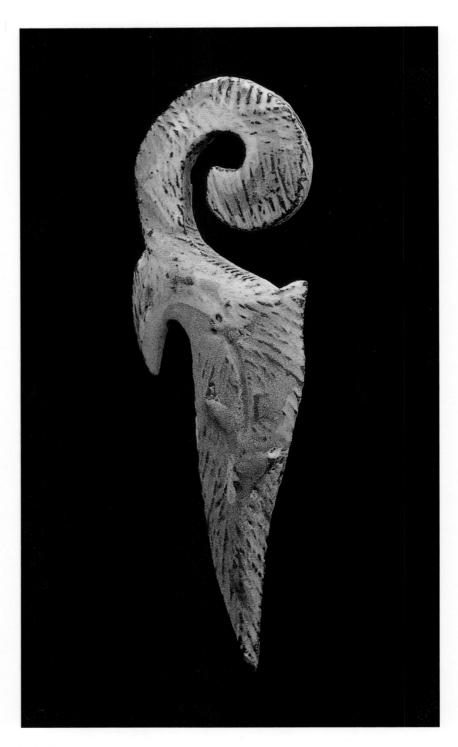

Rocaille #5
Brooch 1992
Enamel, electroformed copper
10cm
Western Australian Centre for the Arts, Perth, Australia

Petrossa #4
Brooch 1992
Enamel, electroformed copper, 14/22ct gold
12cm
Private collection

Petrossa #1
Brooch 1991
Enamel, electroformed copper, 14/22ct gold
10cm
Private collection

Rocaille #11
Brooch 1992
Enamel, electroformed copper
12cm
Western Australian Centre for the Arts, Perth, Australia

Liv Blåvarp

Norway b.1956

Blavarp's large jewellery, made almost entirely of wood and dependent on natural forms, is very body-oriented. There is a strong sense of underlying geometry, but the complex, many-parted approach which she has adopted ensures that the pieces fall back physically onto the body. Their images and overtones of exotic fruitfulness suggest further metaphorical relationships. This work must properly be seen against flesh.

Neckpiece 1990
Birdseye maple, whaletooth, dye
20 × 20cm
Museum of Applied Art, Oslo, Norway

Detail of a neckpiece 1993
Birch, paint, gold leaf
each element c.7cm long
Private collection

Neckpiece 1992
Plane, birch, dye, paint
20 × 20cm
Private collection

Neckpiece "Green bird" 1992
Birch, ebony, paint

Onno Boekhoudt

The Netherlands b. 1944

8 Rings 1989
Sterling silver
2 × 2cm each
Gemeente Museum, Arnhem, The Netherlands

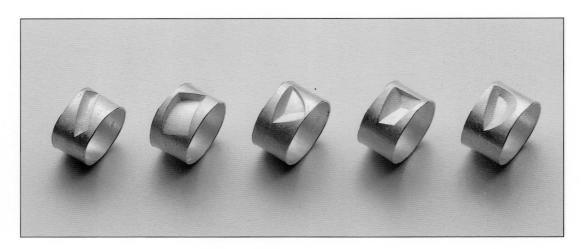

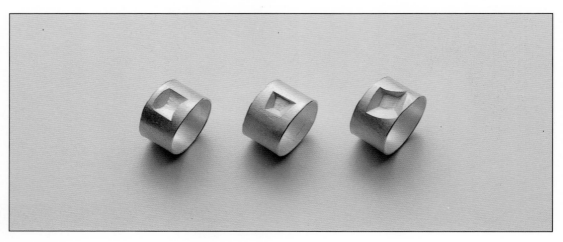

Boekhoudt's jewellery is centred around process – the
phenomena of direct form-finding and form-giving in
which action and object are bound together – rather than
design. It is best revealed when simple. The poetic
economy with which the blows of a tool on metal will
cause a clear, corresponding and particular form to arise is
typical of his aesthetic. His inclination is not to strive for
effect, but to approach his task with undemonstrative
methods and materials.

Brooch 1993
Sterling silver
9 × 5 × 1cm
Private collection

Ring 1990
Sterling silver
22 × 22mm
Hiko Mizuno College of Jewellery, Tokyo, Japan

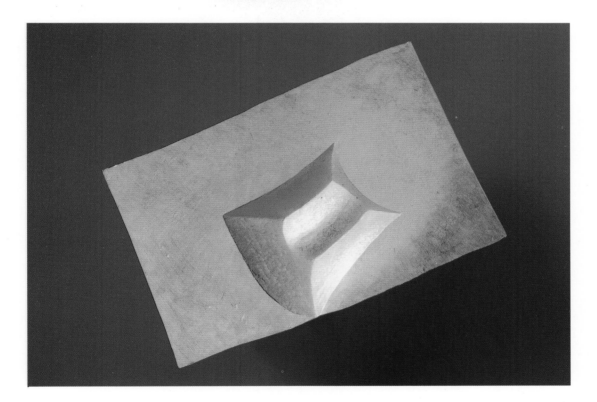

Brooch 1991
Sterling silver
7 × 7.6 × 0.6cm
Gitta van der Donk, Apeldoorn, The Netherlands

Brooch 1993
Sterling silver
8 × 5 × 2cm
Private collection

Rudolf Bott

Germany b.1956

Rings 1991
Rock crystal
Private collection

Bott is unusual in making both jewellery and metalwork (tableware). In spite of their very different cultural and psychological points of departure and arrival, the two subjects share many materials and craft processes, and often intersect on a purely formal basis. It is here that Bott's interest in the expressive characteristics of material and process operates. He deploys sure skill (albeit in a reticent way) and sensibility to pin-point forms which bring out, disclose and explain these characteristics.

Necklace 1989
Fire-gilded brass
Private collection

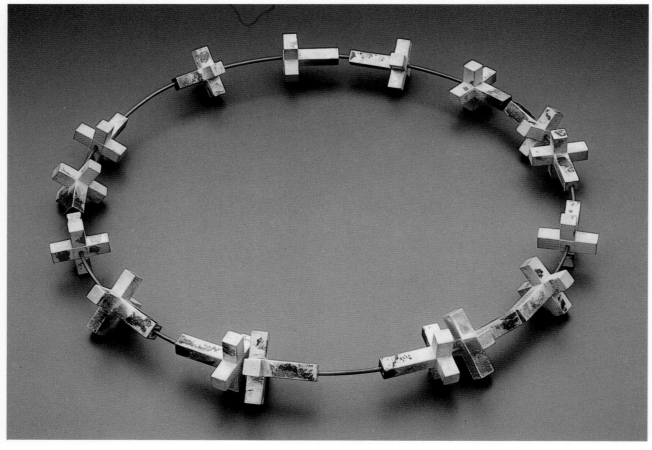

Pins/Brooches 1992
Fire-gilded brass
7 × 5cm
Private collection

Necklace 1989
Silver
Private collection

Joaquim Capdevila

Spain b.1944

Capdevila has been very influential in the development of
Barcelona – where, for instance, he was followed at the
Massana school by Puig Cuyas and Domenech – as the
centre for experimental jewellery in Spain. His later work
seems a little more stripped-down, but still maintains an
irreverent, nonchalant air, still unmistakably Catalan in its
origin and antecedents.

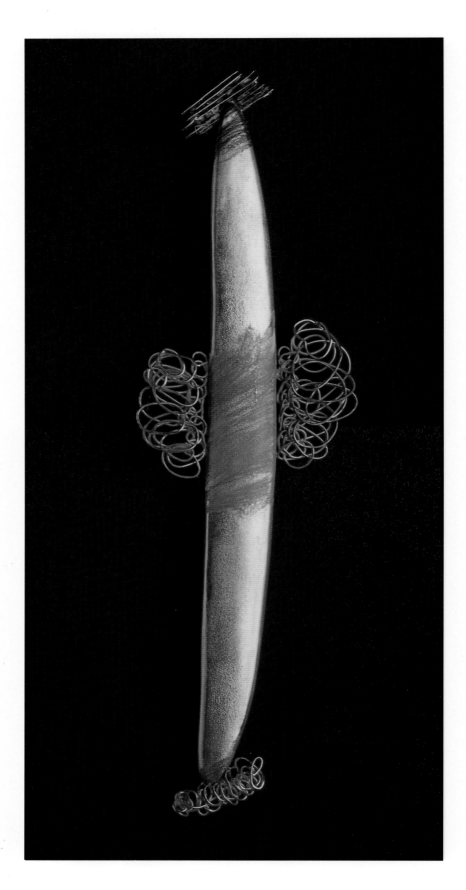

Pin 1993
Silver, gold, acrylic
14.5 × 5cm
Private collection

Mediterraneo
Brooch 1993
Gold, silver, acrylic
6cm (diameter)
Private collection

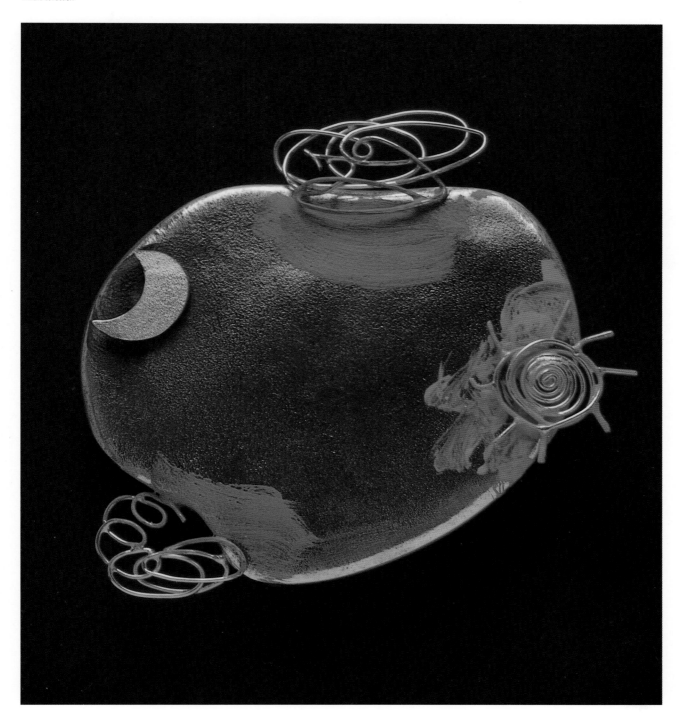

Anton Cepka
Slovakia b.1936

Brooch 1990
Silver, acrylic
7 × 9.5 × 9cm
Private collection

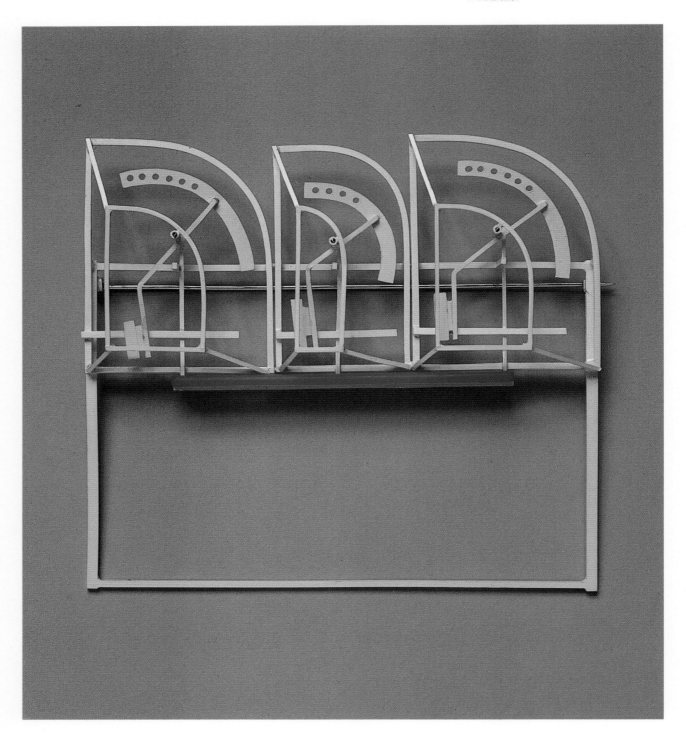

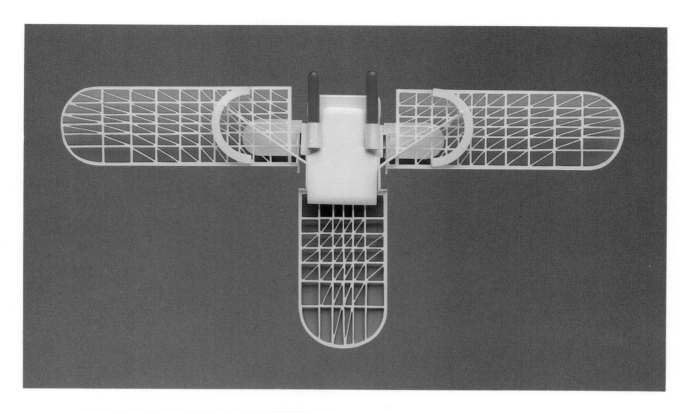

Brooch 1989
Silver, acrylic
Private collection

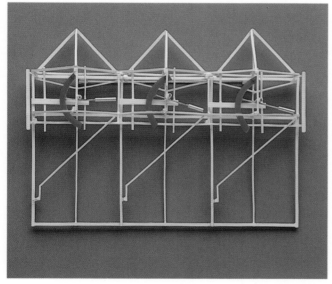

Brooch 1990
Silver, acrylic
6.6 × 8.8 × 1cm
Private collection

These lattice-like constructions are mainly fabricated, but one piece shows Cepka's characteristic technique of piercing from sheet. With these simple means, he has created one of the most complete and memorable visions in contemporary jewellery. Within these beautiful representations of a *Twentieth Century* aesthetic there are, however, traces of automata, of life transfigured, of communications limited to devices, and activity reduced to roboticism. On the other hand their manner of making expresses a tangible humanity.

Peter Chang

UK b.1944

Artists trained in other disciplines have occasionally stepped into the jewellery arena with effect and Chang's virtuoso displays of constructed plastics owe more to his experience in fine art and model-making than to any formal training in jewellery design. His highly ornate and colourful work has also attracted the attention of the fashion world.

Brooch 1992
Acrylic, polyester, lacquer
11 × 5cm
Artist's collection

Bracelet 1993
Acrylic, polyester, PVC, lacquer
15 × 5.5cm
Private collection

Susan Cohn

Australia b.1952

Personal stereos and portable telephones are only the front-runners of a whole world of devices which will have implications for jewellers. *Microphone* represents a series in which Cohn began to explore some aspects of this. She appropriates form and image but discards actual function, ultimately projecting a distancing, decoupling irony and ambiguity. She describes her series *Cosmetic Manipulations* as "the most challenging concept of jewellery I have explored to date". Again, it is the ambiguous relation of small surgical devices to jewellery which she has seen as fertile ground.

Cosmetic Manipulations – Chin
Earring and correction piece 1992
Yellow gold, pink gold, anodised aluminium, rubber
Box: 23 × 16.2 × 1.2cm
Edition of 5
Artist's collection

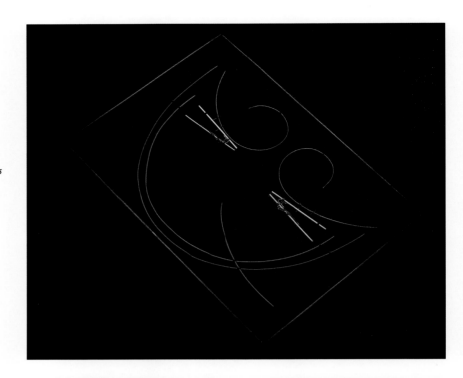

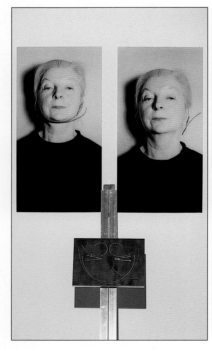

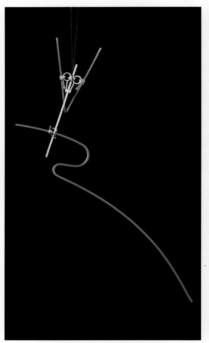

Cosmetic Manipulations – Nose
Brooch (and nose correction piece) 1992
Yellow, gold, pink gold, anodised aluminium
6 × 15cm
Edition of 5
Artist's collection

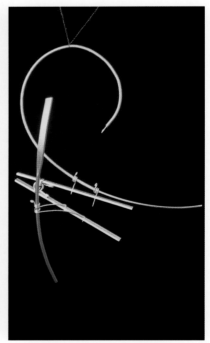

Cosmetic Manipulations – Chin
Earrings 1992
Yellow gold, pink gold, anodised aluminium
Earring piece: 6.5 × 9cm; earring line: 10cm
Edition of 5
Artist's collection

Microphone
Brooch 1990
750 gold, anodised aluminium
5 × 8cm
Edition of 5
Australian National Gallery, Canberra

Cynthia Cousens

UK b.1956

Seeing some of these objects for the first time, it might be surprising to discover that they are rings, so effectively do they resemble hollow vessels. Cousens, having earlier concentrated on a graphic approach – gestural, sometimes pod-like brooches of ornamental line and busy surface – has produced a series of rings which explore themes of encirclement and volume. Ornamentation here is more severely controlled, but typically dark or burnt-in, suggesting associations with ceramic craft, which would confirm its place in an evolving Arts and Crafts tradition.

Rings 1992
Silver, 18ct white gold
2cm (high)
Crafts Council, London/Private collection

Rings 1992
Silver, gold
2cm (high)
Crafts Council, London/Private collection

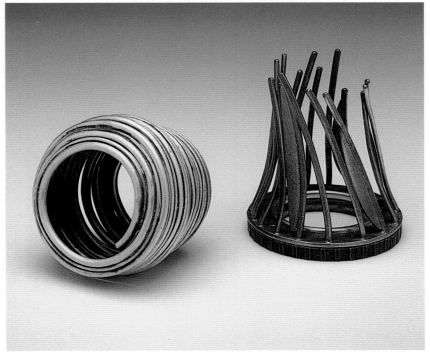

Cocoon and *Whisper* rings 1993
Silver, gold
2cm (high)
Artist's collection

Georg Dobler

Germany b.1952

Dobler explores some similarities, differences and common ground between "found" and fabricated structures, enjoying the ambiguities of nature and artifice. The translation of organic materials into metal, by casting, enables him to develop this aesthetic, and the delicacy of these captured elements contributes to their particular character, but one only has to imagine them polished to understand the effects of their subtle treatment. Dobler's work is always light and airy: insubstantiality is an underlying theme, and it imparts a particular nuance to the idea of "precious".

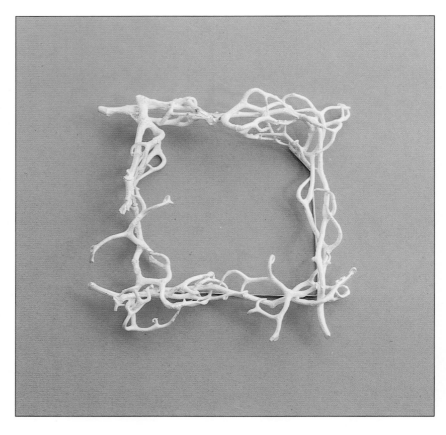

Brooch 1990
Silver
9 × 8cm
Private collection

Brooch 1991
Silver
9 × 10cm
Private collection

Brooch 1989
Steel and gold wire
16 × 9 × 2cm
Private collection

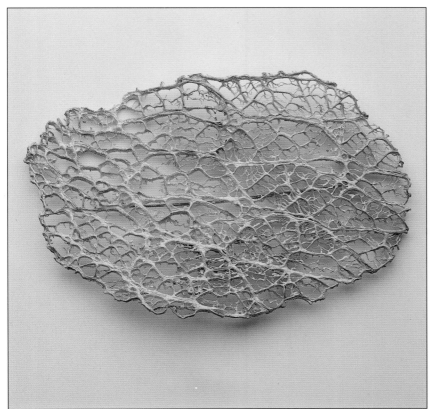

Brooch 1990
Silver
14 × 11cm
Private collection

Xavier Domenech

Spain b.1960

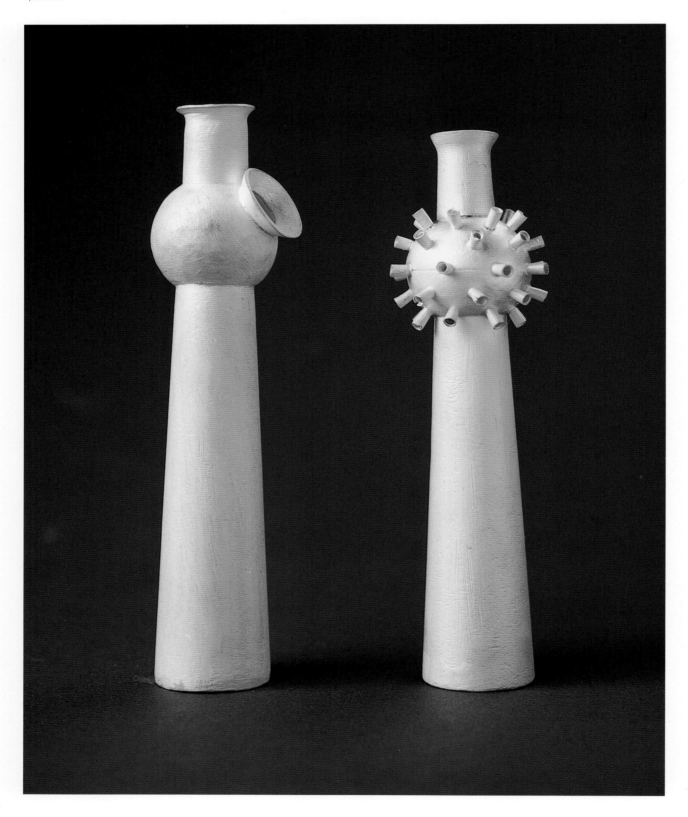

Matagi
Brooch 1992
Patinated copper, silver
10 × 2 × 2cm
Artist's collection

Nook
Brooch 1993
Silver, bronze, steel
7 × 7.5 × 1cm
Artist's collection

Soma
Brooch 1993
Patinated bronze, silver
8.5 × 3 × 3cm
Artist's collection

Domenech's theme is containment. Like a number of other contemporary jewellers, he seeks, through the form and treatment of his work, a special connection with the mysteries of a more rudimentary culture – the craftsman as magician. This motive tests the artist's ability to summon up objects with spirit, and this is consistent with his view of the jewel as an object which somehow connects the inner and outer worlds.

Venus Sativa I and *Venus Sativa II*
Brooches 1993
Silver
9 × 2.5 × 2.5cm; 8.5 × 2.5 × 2.5cm
Artist's collection

Jacomÿm van der Donk

The Netherlands b. 1963

Rings which relate to the inside of the hand – thereby addressing the wearer more than the observer might realise – occur from time to time, but rarely with so much emphasis. Such rings can give secret and surreptitious pleasure to the one who knows, but these are more overt. Their hidden secrets have become their dominant and visible motive. They deal in sensation – texture, movement, sound, weight – but openly, revealing or signalling some aspect of the wearer as a sensuous being.

Bracelet 1993
Silver, hair, stone, mirror
35cm
Private collection

Ring 1993
Silver, hair
7cm
Private collection

Ring 1993
Ivory, gold, pearl, glass
12cm
Private collection

Ring 1992
Silver
5cm
Private collection

Arline M. Fisch
USA b.1931

Fisch has been active and instrumental at a national and
international level for many years, teaching, organizing
and contributing to significant events and exhibitions. An
astute craftswoman, she has pioneered processes which
bring softness and pliability to metals. Her latest works,
which have always been designed to "enhance and exalt"
the wearer, are based typically on textile structures.

Black and White Plaid #1
Necklace 1992
Sterling silver, 18ct gold, plaited
35 × 42.5cm
Artist's collection

Gerda Flöckinger

UK b.1927

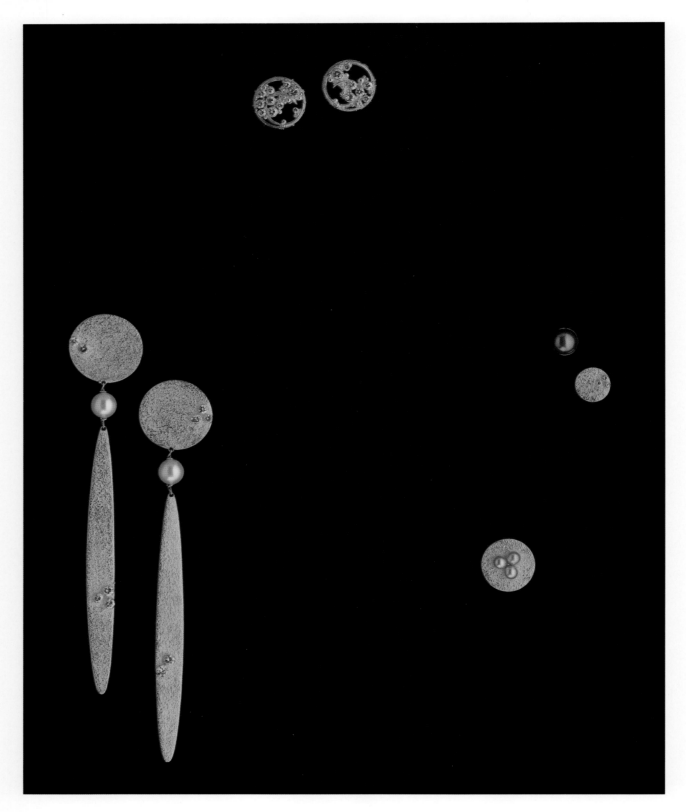

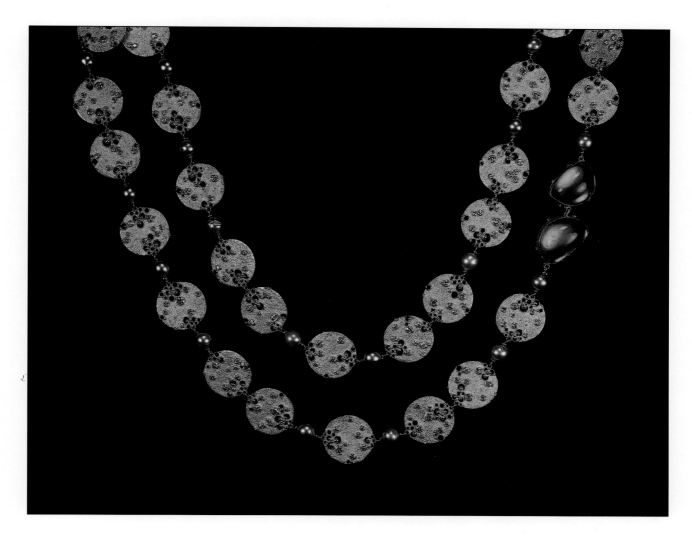

Neckpiece

18ct gold, diamonds, amber, oxidised silver, blue cultured pearls

An early protagonist of artist-jewellery in Britain, Flöckinger pursues her own highly developed technique of gold fusion and erosion. This controlled enrichment of surface, allied to precious and semi-precious stones – and, most sympathetically, to pearls – produces a unique and immediately recognizable style. The ear pieces illustrate a development in which any combination or number of parts may be worn at once, depending on the number of piercings.

Ear pieces 1993

18ct gold, diamonds, pearl

Pendants: 97 × 18mm; studs 13mm (diameter); black pearl: 6.5mm (diameter); three-pearl piece: 13mm (diameter); small stud: 9mm (diameter)

Private collection, Hong Kong

Lisa Gralnick

USA b.1956

Gralnick's black pieces were made between 1985 and 1989. Their fragmentation and their immediately sinister and mechanistic forms are compounded by zoomorphic undertones, and yet they remain essentially a celebration of acrylic. Acrylic is one of the "discoveries" of contemporary jewellery, and the material can project a seductiveness which is all its own, rewarding reverent and precise handling with a quality which is at once defined and yielding.

Bracelet 1987
Constructed acrylic (14ct gold mechanism)
9 × 11.5 × 7.5cm
Stedelijk Museum, Amsterdam, The Netherlands

Brooch 1988
Constructed acrylic
15 × 5 × 4cm
Robert Pfannebecker

Brooch 1987
Constructed acrylic
18 × 4 × 2.5cm
Private collection

William Harper

USA b.1944

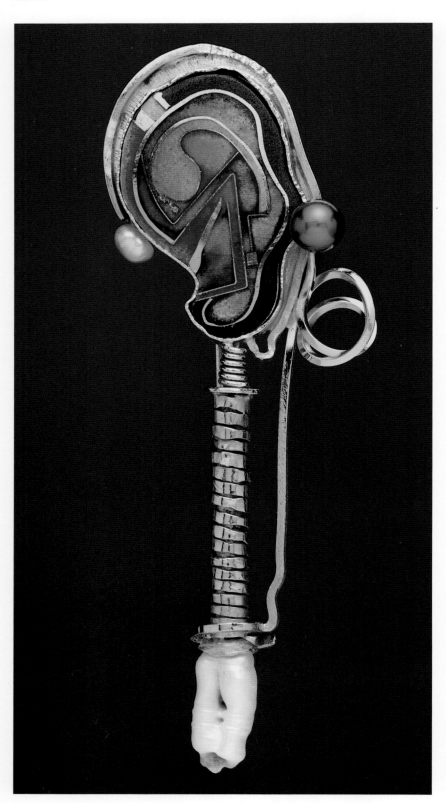

Enamelling amounts to a separate category, or sub-set, of jewellery. Within it Harper is an outstanding individualist. That he has great command of his craft is quite clear, and yet he appears to eschew technique, and can be casual with metals. This sometimes controversial and inevitably paradoxical position is one which should be well understood by many other jewellery artists. It stems from Harper's determination that the expressive and subjective impact of his ideas should not be qualified by concerns of craft.

Ripe Blossom II
Brooch
Gold cloisonné enamel on fine silver and gold, opals, pearls
8.4 × 5.2 × 1.5cm
Artist's collection

Grotesque self-portrait of the Artist as the Goddess Kali
Brooch 1990
Gold cloisonné enamel on fine silver and gold, opal, pearl, moonstones
10.2 × 7.7 × 3cm
Artist's collection

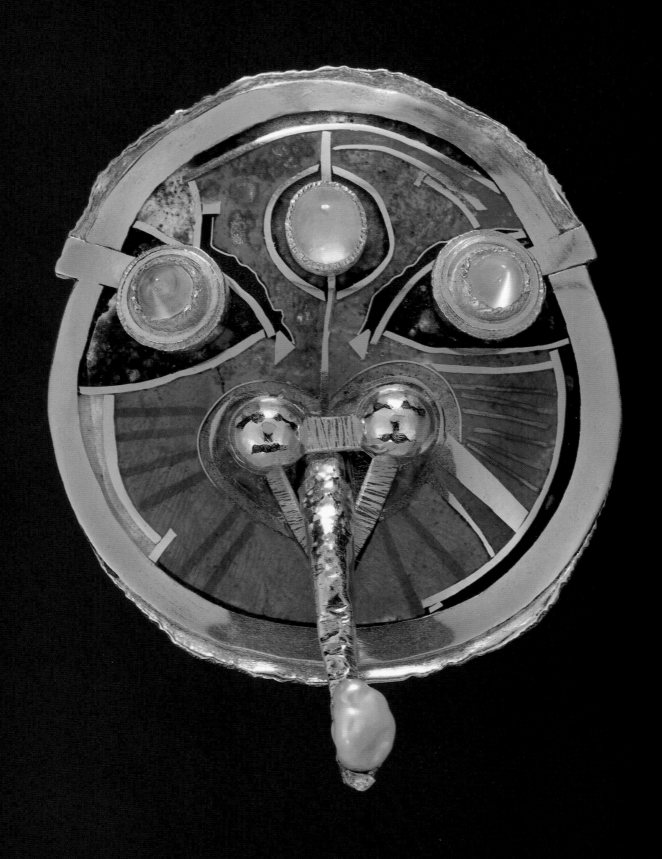

Self-portrait of the Artist as a Haruspex
Brooch 1990
Gold cloisonné enamel on fine silver and gold, opals, coral, shell
29.4 × 6.5 × 4.8cm
National Museum of American Art, Washington DC, USA

Fabergé's Seed #7
Brooch 1993
Gold cloisonné enamel on fine silver and gold, pearls
11.9 × 8cm
Artist's collection

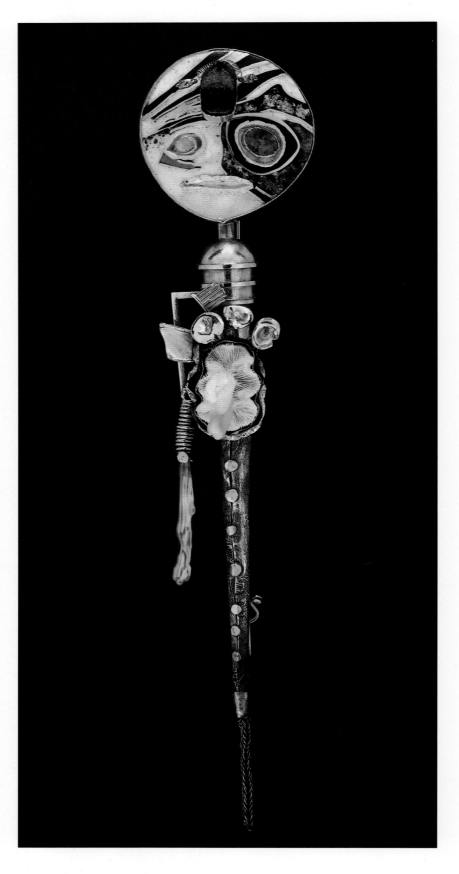

Anna Heindl

Austria b.1950

Heindl's jewellery is first of all good to wear, but it is not completely submissive. It has a certain tough angularity of style, which is underlined by the use of faceted stones. She has persisted in the use of semi-precious stones through a period in which most artist-jewellers would have rejected them, and has succeeded in keeping them in place as compositional elements. She thus alludes to Deco excess, while projecting a more stringent, modern tone.

Tüten/Bags
Necklace 1992
18ct gold, silver, amethyst
42cm long
Private collection

Ohr/Ear
Brooch 1991
18ct gold, tourmaline, topaz
6.5 × 3.5cm
Private collection

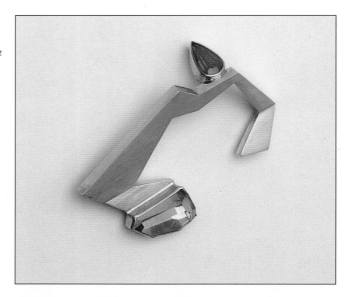

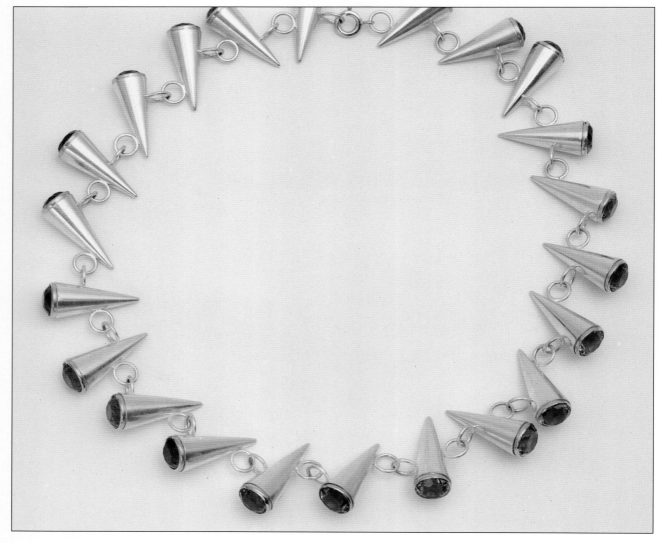

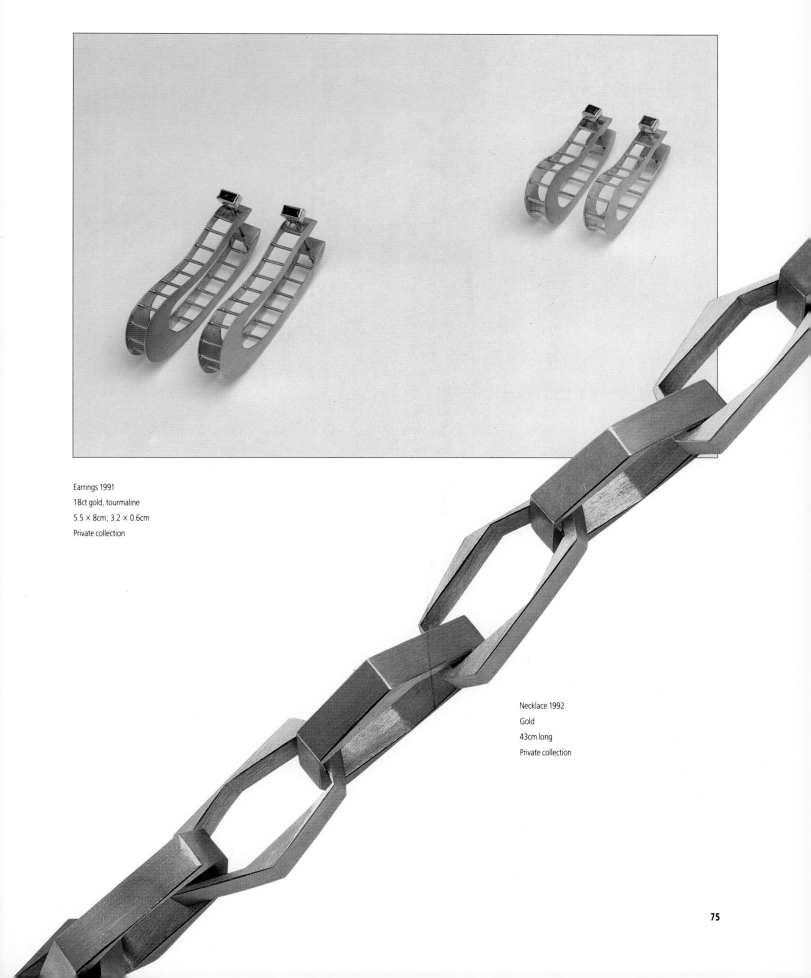

Earrings 1991
18ct gold, tourmaline
5.5 × 8cm; 3.2 × 0.6cm
Private collection

Necklace 1992
Gold
43cm long
Private collection

Therese Hilbert

Germany b.1948

Hilbert's jewellery celebrates the ambiguities of modest and clear form. It embodies a perception of jewellery as a language – almost Masonic, addressing a privileged circle – of private signs and tokens, which are to be recognised as such, and yet remain quite enigmatic. The pieces are simply made, yet with the assurance of a technical command which can undermine, or conceal, their complexity.

Brooch 1991
Silver
8.2 × 4.3cm
Artist's collection

Brooch 1992
Silver
8.5 × 6.4 × 2.4cm
Artist's collection

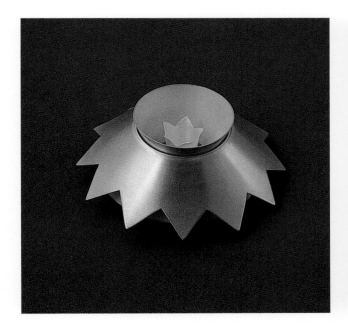

Brooch 1992
Silver
7.5 × 2.8cm
Artist's collection

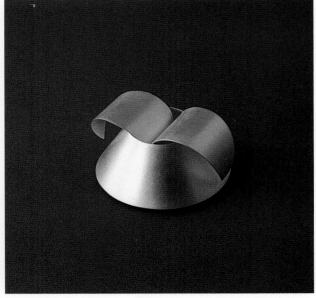

Brooch b.1991
Silver
5.5 × 2.8cm
Artist's collection

Brooch 1992
Silver
7.5 × 6.3 × 2.4cm
Artist's collection

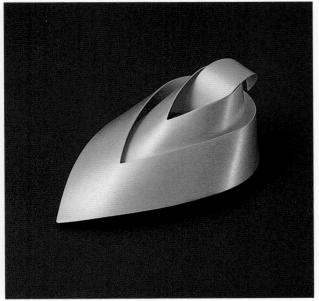

Brooch 1991
Silver
11 × 7 × 4cm
Farago Foundation, USA

Yasuki Hiramatsu

Japan b.1926

Bracelet 1992
Fine gold, resin, gold leaf
9.5 × 4.8cm
Private collection

Although there was jewellery in Japan in ancient times, it
had, until quite recently, been lost to the culture.
Hiramatsu has been a prime mover in the development of
Japanese contemporary jewellery. His own work has gone
through many phases, building always upon knowledge
and experience of traditional metalworking, to create a
contemporary oeuvre of great dignity. Where some
craftsmen would seek to impress with abundance and
complexity, Hiramatsu has repeatedly affirmed the simple
strengths of restraint, sensibility and wit.

Necklace 1989
Silver
31 × 21 × 8cm
Private collection

Wahei Ikezawa

Japan b.1946

These strong works by Ikezawa ought perhaps to be called "bodypieces", since the neck is used only as an anchor, or point of departure. They are a narrative of the constituent parts, in the manner of unfolding a story. This reading of them is emphasised by the more-or-less linear arrangement, which, in its orderly progression from one part to the next, also enforces a strict formality.

Regenerat
Neckpiece 1991
Iron, brass, copper, hemp
80 × 10cm
Private collection

Regenerat
Neckpiece 1991
Iron, brass, wood
75 × 43cm
Private collection

Kazuhiro Itoh

Japan b.1948

In Itoh's work, expression of the aesthetic character of the material is always critical. He assembles these neckpieces informally, like collected bird feathers or chippings found on a forest floor. The equally unforced and somehow tentative conjunction with steel wire is acutely judged. The bronze pieces are, by contrast, made like signs and eloquently liquid.

Necklace 1992
Wood, steel
30cm (diameter)
Private collection

Necklace 1992
Wood, steel
35cm (diameter)
Private collection

Bracelet, pendant, ring 1991
Bronze
Box: 50 × 50cm
Private collection

Gilles Jonemann

France b.1944

Jonemann exploits papier mâché with great finesse. Occasionally used for non-precious experiments, this material has a range of expression which is very sympathetic to jewellery. Some of Jonemann's pieces are so large or sculptural that they must be carried, and can only be categorized as "jewellery" at a stretch, but the pieces illustrated here are fine-tuned for appeal and wearability.

Necklace 1990
Papier mâché
Private collection

Brooch 1988
Papier mâché
20cm
Private collection

Hermann Jünger

Germany b.1928

Brooch 1992

Silver, champlevé enamel

6cm (diameter)

Artist's collection

A significant artist, following his appointment to the Academy in Munich, Jünger became one of the most influential teachers in the recent history of jewellery. He has followed the line that jewellery cannot become "fine art" by borrowing from the other arts, but must achieve this status from within its own special character and agendas – a difficult line, but a critical challenge. In these works, with their unforced but knowing animation of surface, their undemonstrative, somewhat archaic richness and their secure judgment of internal scale, Jünger deploys effortless control.

3 Brooches 1992
Gold, silver, enamel
Artist's collection

3 Brooches 1992
Silver, enamel
Artist's collection

2 Pendants 1990
Fine gold on silver, iron, tombac
6 × 5cm; 4 × 55cm
Artist's collection

Svatopluk Kasaly

Czech Republic b.1944

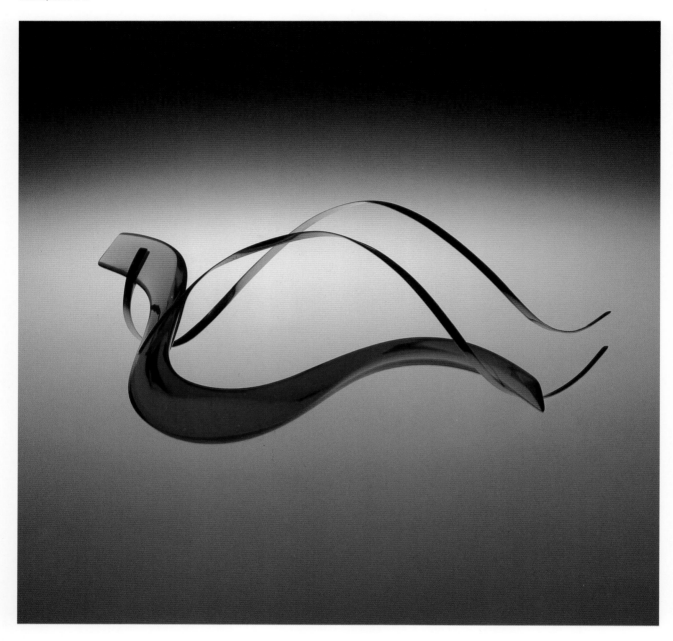

Necklace 1991

35 × 22 × 14cm

Private collection

A jeweller and sculptor of glass for architecture, Kasaly comes from a region of the Czech Republic which has strong traditions in both disciplines. In the jewellery illustrated here, the direct and eloquent simplicity with which glass and metal are joined, and the liquid elegance of line and form, are hallmarks of Kasaly's style, but the true revelation of his intentions is in the wearing. The transaction, or transposition of sensuous attributes between the materials and the wearer is unmistakable.

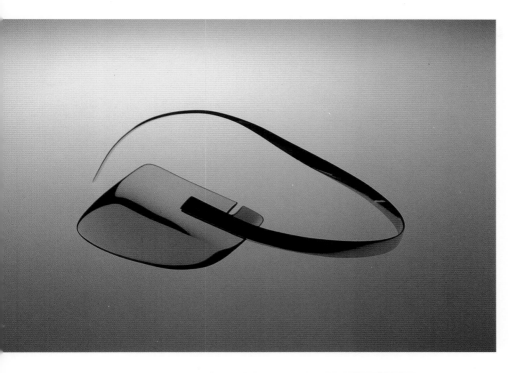

Necklace 1991
Brass, nickel, rhodium, cut glass
23 × 16 × 7cm
Private collection

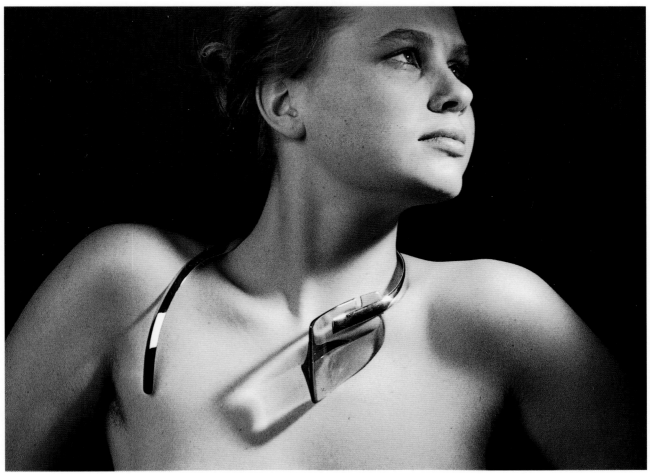

Daniel Kruger

Germany b.1951

Ring 1992

Silver, rubelite, rubies, emeralds

2 × 1.4 × 3.2cm

Artist's collection

Ring 1993

Gold, peridots, cornelian

3 × 4 × 3cm

Artist's collection

Ring 1993

Silver, amethyst, emeralds, rubies

4 × 2.3 × 2.5cm

Artist's collection

Kruger is one of the most consistently inventive goldsmiths of his generation. This collection shows only rings, and they are clearly historicist in intention, but his output has included all kinds of jewellery in materials as diverse as feathers, silks and broken glass, owing little to current trends. He also works as a ceramic artist. Unforced, but always thoughtful, feeling and questioning, his work is touched by serenity and serendipity.

Ring 1993
Gold, topaz
4 × 2.5cm
Artist's collection

Winfried Krüger

Germany b.1944

Krüger, like many of his colleagues, is a fully-trained and
experienced goldsmith, but chooses to underplay the grounding
factuality of goldsmith's craft in order to release ambiguity,
placing his wearable objects in a more mythic location of
uncertain scale. Washed in white plaster as if in moonlight, they
seem at once complete and yet fragmented.

Abschied von Berlin/Farewell to Berlin
Brooch 1990–91
Silver, plaster
15cm
Private collection, made to commission

Faust
Brooch 1990–91
Silver, plaster
12 × 12cm
Private collection

Wenn ich ein Röslein wär/If I were a small rose
Brooch 1990–91
Silver, iron, plaster
15 × 17cm
Private collection

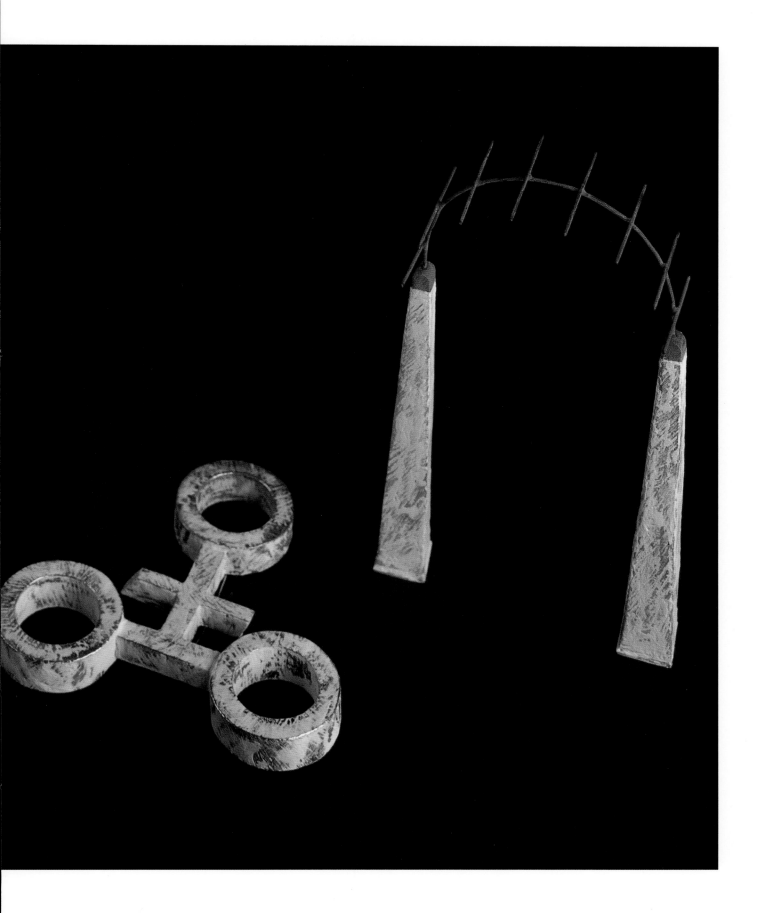

Otto Künzli

Germany b.1948

This work stems from Künzli's visits to the USA, where from local subject matter he made observations on culture in general, and the culture of jewellery in particular. His work can be playful, even mischievous. He manages very well the shock of the banal (a Dada strategy) and a sense of ironic detachment – with which, of course, he contrives to be at once "insider" and "outsider". His work is, however, firmly rooted in the craft of jewellery: always meticulously made; thoughtfully and fastidiously presented.

Oh, say!
Brooch 1991
Gold
9 × 9 × 0.6cm
Farago Foundation, USA

Black Mickey Mouse
Brooch 1991
Hard foam, lacquer, steel
9.3 × 10 × 4.5cm
Artist's collection

UFO – Unidentified Found Objects
Pendants 1992
Rusted iron, gold
10 × 20 × 0.2cm (13 pieces)
Artist's collection

1492 – When Mickey Mouse was born
Shoulder piece – 1992
Silicate
6 × 4.5 × 4.5cm
Françoise van den Bosch Stichting

Stanley Lechtzin

USA b.1936

SWPTORC.TIFF
Neckpiece 1994
CAD/CAM virtual for acrylic and gold
25.5 × 25.5cm

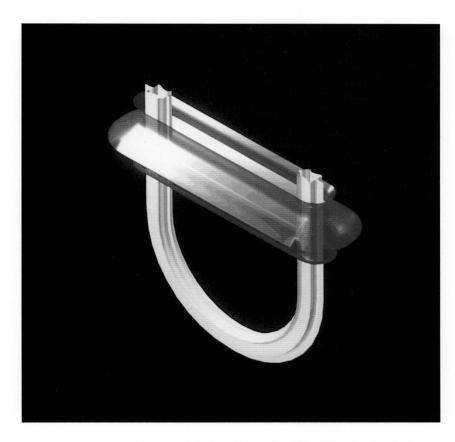

Lechtzin is justly celebrated for his earlier researches into electroforming, with which he produced some extraordinary and challenging jewellery. He has recently entered the technological area of CAD/CAM (computer aided design and manufacturing), confident that its processes will open up new aesthetic horizons. These objects are not "real", but they exist as a set of instructions, which is arguably only a small step away. The images prefigure rather than record the pieces, but this is perhaps less immediately important than the vocabularies of form which become grist for the artist's mill.

PENTSPLC.TIF
Bracelet 1992
CAD/CAM virtual for acrylic and gold
10 × 10cm

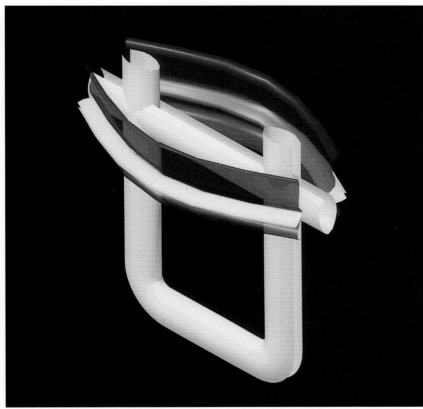

XBRACE.TIF
Bracelet 1992
CAD/CAM virtual for acrylic and gold
10 × 12.5cm

Mary Lee Hu

USA b.1943

Some artists need to move on quickly. Others find a
particular area of research so absorbing that they dig in
deeper and longer. Lee Hu's experiments in the transfer of
textile or fibre to metal techniques have been pursued
consistently, through many phases, over many years. She
has gone on to amass one of the most coherent and
satisfying oeuvres in the whole field.

Choker #80
Neckpiece 1992
18/22ct gold – twined and constructed
18.5 × 18.8 × 1cm
Artist's collection

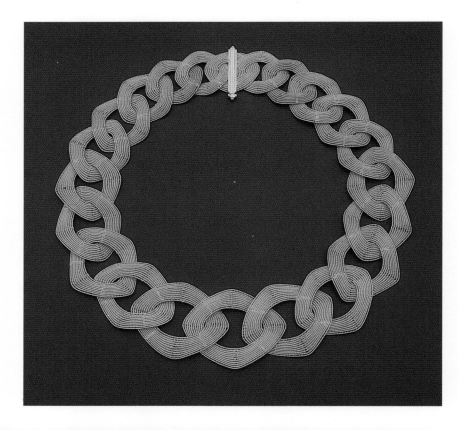

Choker #78
Neckpiece 1991
18/22ct gold – twined and constructed
16.2 × 22.5 × 3.8cm
Artist's collection

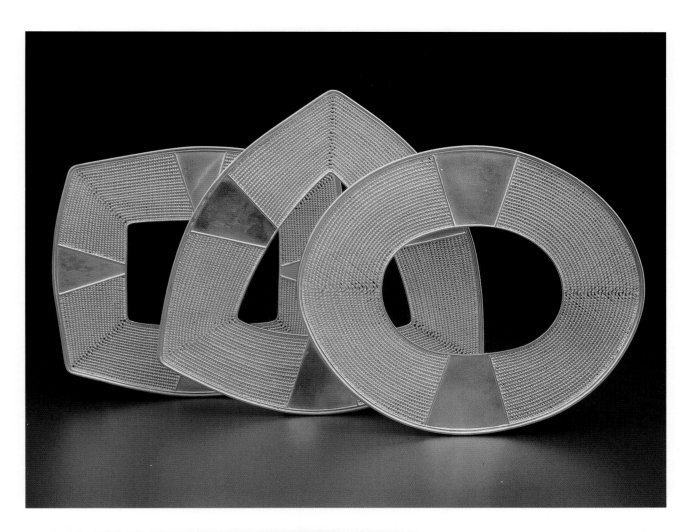

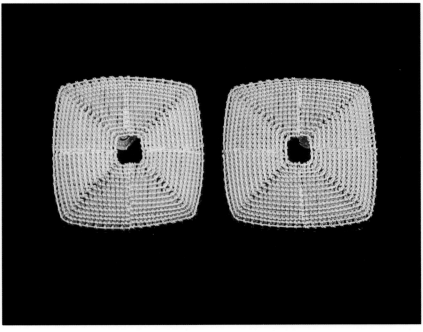

Bracelets #43, 44, 45
1989
18/22ct gold – twined and constructed
14 × 14 × 0.3cm max.
Private collection

Earrings #136
1990
18/22ct gold – twined and constructed
3.8 × 3.8cm
Artist's collection

Jens-Rüdiger Lorenzen

Germany b.1942

Lorenzen's complex constructions contrive to express spontaneity together with painstaking selectivity. The process of assemblage is typical of his approach. A highly developed sensitivity to materials brings together a rich array of visual and tactile sensations. In this way – if not conventionally – some important requirements of jewellery are satisfied. He has often treated jewellery as miniature sculpture, but more usually – through brooches – in relief. Here he seems to revel in the spatial freedom which a ring can more readily offer.

Legende No 9
Brooch 1992
Steel, argentan, paper collage, varnish
5 × 8cm
Artist's collection

Brooch 1992
Steel, argentan, paper
6 × 7.5cm
Artist's collection

Ring 1992
Steel, argentan, paper
3.5 × 4cm
Artist's collection

Ring 1992
Steel, argentan
5.5 × 5cm
Artist's collection

Fritz Maierhofer

Austria b.1941

Ring 1991
Yellow and white gold
7.3 × 5.5cm
Private collection

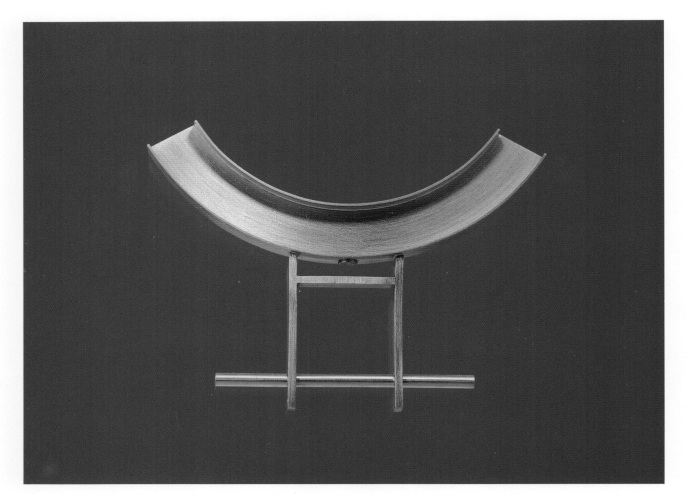

One of the outstanding artist-goldsmiths of his generation, Maierhofer's skills give him an enviable ability to deceive – to create faultless objects with no sense of struggle. Aware of the potentially suffocating effects of tradition, he freed himself first by experiments in multi-coloured acrylic, then tin, and so on, always looking for new opportunities and always with precious metals playing an essential role. These new works owe something to an earlier series developed from steel building construction, as well as to post-modernism and Vienna.

Brooch 1991
Yellow and white gold, amethyst, citrine, rubelite, diamonds
10.6 × 7.9cm
Private collection

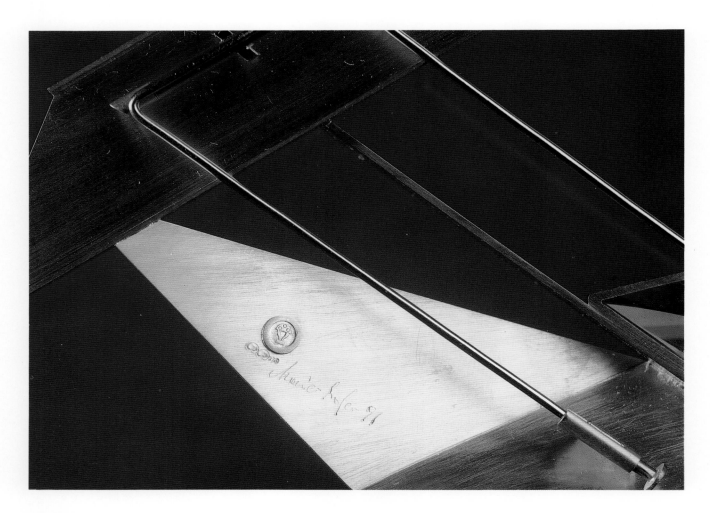

Detail of Brooch

Brooch 1991
Yellow and white gold, amethyst
8.1 × 10.1cm
Private collection

Carlier Makigawa

Canada/Australia b.1952

The space-frame approach of the two brooches is typical of Makigawa. In these pieces the sometimes tense, sometimes undulating wires and soft surfaces describe transparent vessels which exist somewhere between artefact and organism. To bring together complex resonances, which in this case take in Hellenic ornament and marine biology, contributes to the success of a piece of jewellery.

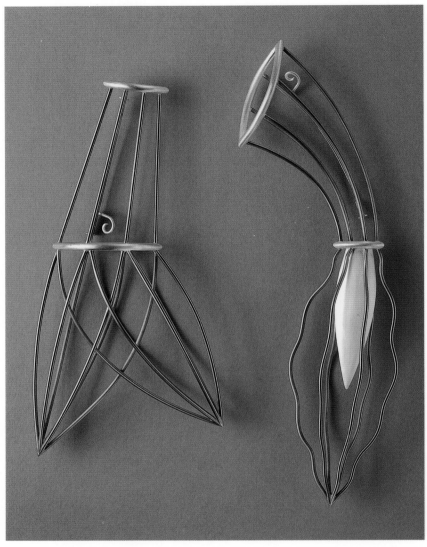

2 Brooches 1991
Silver, monel metal
13cm long
Edition of 3
Private collection

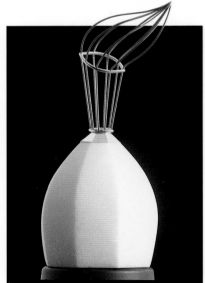

Object 1992
Silver, monel metal, marble
30 × 12 × 12cm
Private collection

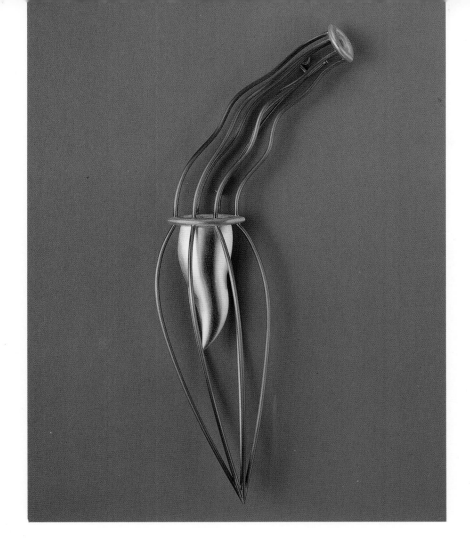

Brooch 1991
Repoussé silver, monel metal
17 × 4 × 2.5cm
Edition of 3
National Gallery of Victoria, Melbourne

2 Rings/objects
Silver, monel metal, marble
12 × 7.5 × 4.5cm
Private collection

Bruno Martinazzi

Italy b.1923

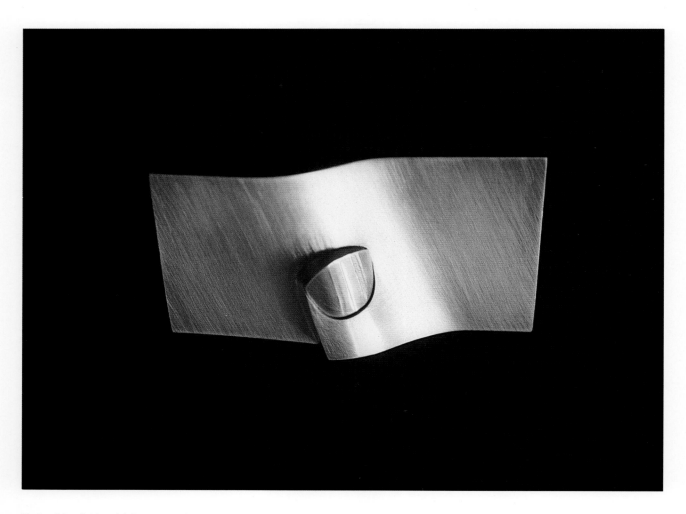

Martinazzi's jewellery is made by hammering and punching thin sheets of metal into shape. It is itself an ancient practice, and these svelte and idealised anatomical fragments are at once classical and votive. The wearing of such body fragments turns a psychic screw which is particular to jewellery. They bear eloquent testimony to the responsive warmth of gold, and their aura of magic is as much due to the rapt perfection with which they are formed as to their symbolic and cultural resonances. They remain ambiguous.

Epistemy
Brooch 1993
18ct gold
6.8 × 3.8cm
Artist's collection

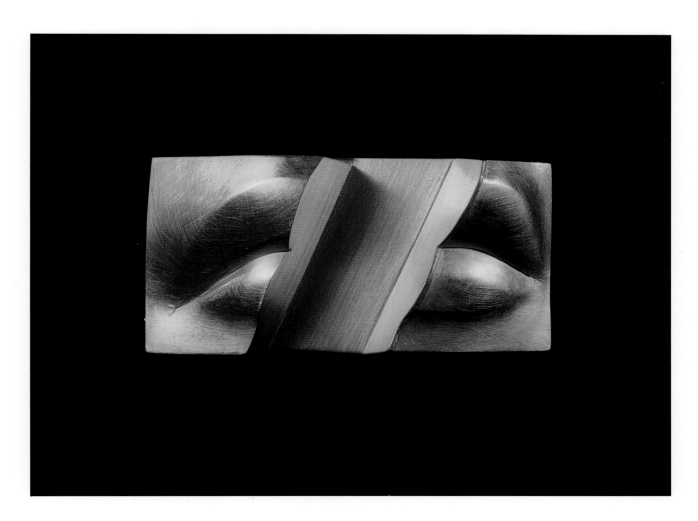

Kaos
Brooch 1992
18/20ct gold
6.5 × 3.5cm
Artist's collection

Metamorphosis
Bracelet 1992
18/20ct yellow and white gold
7.5 × 6cm
Artist's collection

Reversibility
Bracelet 1992
18/20ct white and yellow gold
7 × 3.8cm
Artist's collection

Wilhelm T. Mattar

Germany b.1946

Ring 1989
18ct gold, mother-of-pearl
4 × 11 × 1.5cm
Private collection

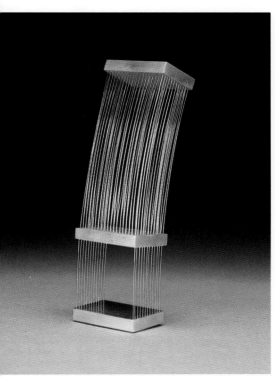

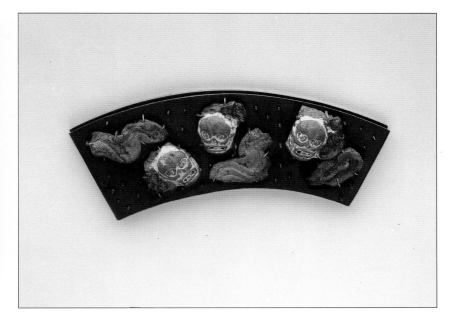

Lift
Ring 1985
18ct gold, stainless steel
7 × 2 × 1.5cm
Schmuckmuseum, Pforzheim

One can no longer make assumptions about the appropriate subject matter of jewellery and Mattar illustrates here something of the breadth of his own. In some cases the character of materials provides a basic agenda. In others, materials are either in the service of narrative ideas or at least interdependent with them. Different though they are, both types are quite representative of his approach, which is always thoughtful and often takes surprising turns.

Brooch 1987
Brass, gold, terracotta
9 × 3.5 × 1cm
Private collection

Brooch 1991
Silver, 18ct gold
8 × 5 × 1cm
Artist's collection

Bruce Metcalf

USA b.1949

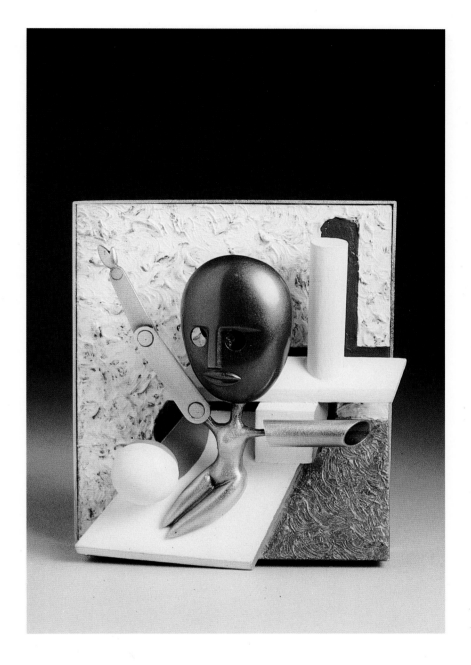

The strength of Metcalf's work – and that of many
American craftsmen – is its affirmative cry. Although one
can interpret his message very literally as a rant – a rage
against the ineffectualness of art and artists – it also strikes
a rhetorical blow for freedom from approved orthodoxies.
These exist even in jewellery. American contemporary
jewellery has its own history, being unafraid to address
issues on a very broad front. Metcalf's singular and
disturbing images of the artist as antic outsider are very
telling.

Wood Pin #57
Pin 1990
Maple, brass, lead, paint, bronze powders, silicon carbide
12.7 × 8.9cm
Private collection

Manfred Nisslmüller

Austria b.1940

A goldsmith, and winner of a Diamond International Award, Nisslmüller tests expectation with irony and economy. Each piece addresses jewellery itself. The ring celebrates archetypical simplicity of form with archetypical beauty of material, but it has spun itself out so far that it can no longer be worn. "Acoustic Jewellery" connects the wearing of images (and the satisfaction of self-image) with the carrying around of one's own selected sound aura. The black isolation room (including surveillance slot) of the "Brooch for a Brooch", with its themes of imprisonment, concealment and perhaps morbid curiosity, is characteristically probing: will the "real jewellery" ever escape?

Fur eine Brosche/For a Brooch
Brooch for a Brooch 1993
Brass, steel, varnish
6 × 3.7cm
Private collection

Fur den schönen Finger/For the beautiful finger
Ring 1989/90
Fine gold
10 × 3.7 × 1.7cm
Private collection

Taschenrecorder/Portable stereo
Accoustic jewellery 1985–93
Microcassette recorder
11 × 5.2 × 1.8cm
Private collection

Johannes Oppermann

Germany b.1960

Ring 1991
Compressed wood, gold
7 × 6 × 2.2cm
Private collection

Ring 1993
Tin sheet
7 × 3.5 × 3cm
Private collection

Opperman defines his working method as "play with
materials, forms and dimensions". The first of these is
evidently the most important. It leads into a recurring
theme of contemporary jewellery: the aesthetic upgrading
of relatively humble (Opperman, interestingly, uses the
word "profane") materials. This is achieved by elaboration,
skill and transference to more precious purposes.

Ring 1991
Compressed wood, gold
7 × 5.5 × 2.2cm
Private collection

Ring 1993
Tin sheet
5.5 × 3.5 × 3.5cm
Private collection

Ring 1993
Tin sheet
6 × 4 × 3cm
Private collection

Barbara Paganin

Italy b.1961

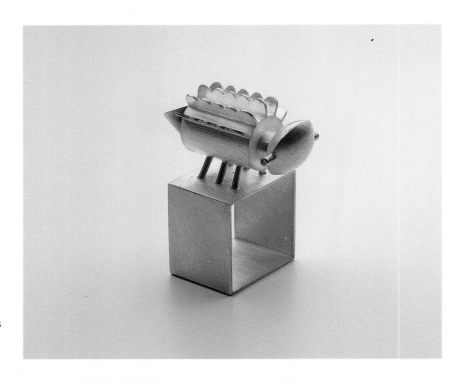

Microftalmo
Ring 1993
18ct gold, silver, jade, diamonds
3.6 × 3.3 × 1.9cm
Private collection

Radiolari
Rings 1992
18ct gold, silver, niello, diamonds
c. 3 × 3 × 1.5cm
Private collection

Paganin's constructions hover uncertainly between the brutal forms of renaissance warfare and the cute fantasy robotics of Hollywood. The pieces carry an air of contrivance and threat, which their robust – it is tempting to say, "barbaric" – ornamentation only enhances. This reflects very well a fundamental and historic image of goldsmithery – of cunning and indispensable service to the sometimes secret purposes of others.

Pteri Gota
Bracelet 1993
18ct gold, diamonds
8.5 × 2.9 × 7.5cm
Private collection

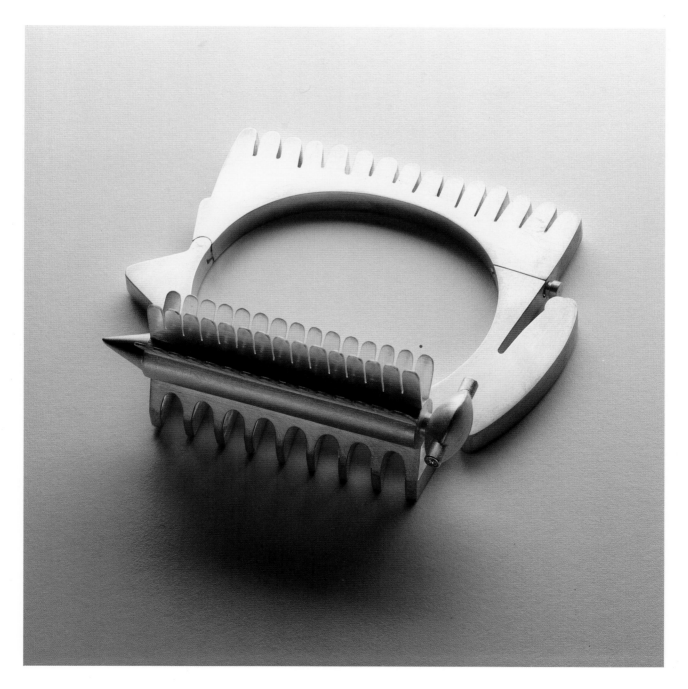

Francesco Pavan

Italy b.1937

Pavan makes jewellery of great subtlety and delicacy, conceived to celebrate the qualities of gold. His intersecting planes, in flattened perspective, are built from different colours of gold such that they represent the strata of a flimsy architecture or the chromatic tones of a breathy sound. They are formally strong – simple, unrefined – and yet the metal becomes, like paper, insubstantial and vulnerable, which only serves to underline its intrinsic preciousness.

Vibrazioni cromatiche
Brooch 1992
18ct red, yellow, green gold
15 × 8 × 1cm
Artist's collection

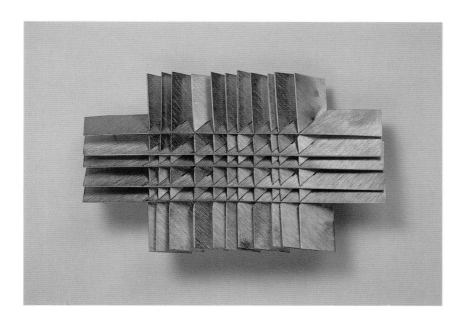

Vibrazioni cromatiche
Brooch 1992
18ct red, yellow, green gold
8 × 5 × 1cm
Artist's collection

Vibrazioni cromatiche
Brooch 1992
18ct red, yellow, green gold
10 × 10 × 1cm
Artist's collection

Ruudt Peters

The Netherlands b.1950

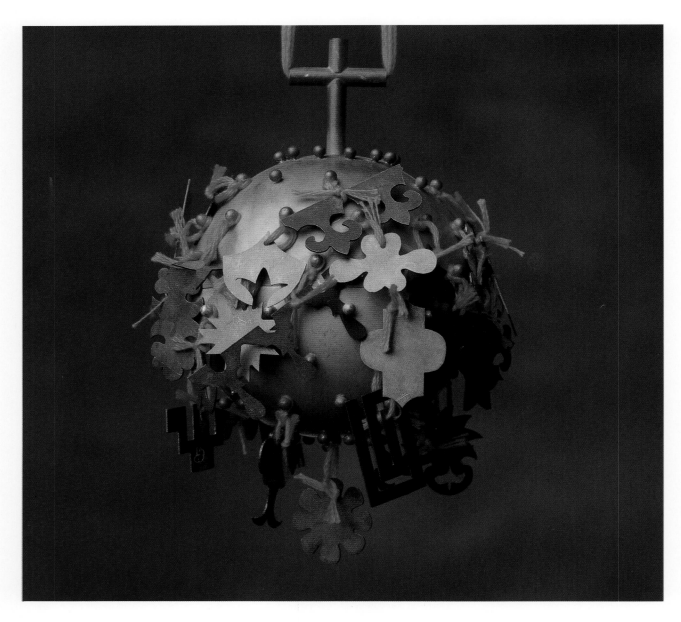

The chain, as a form, is not sufficiently explored by contemporary jewellers, yet it has a great sensual and associative potential. With his "Passio" series of vessel-form pendants – generally dark and dramatic invocations of figures from history or mythology – Peters catches very acutely the tones of religion, eroticism and decadence. In all these pieces, the chains are perhaps the most telling and eloquent parts.

Maciavelli
Neckpiece 1992
Patinated silver, silk
7 × 7 × 11cm
Private collection

Antinöus
Neckpiece 1992
Patinated silver, black pearls
47 × 47 × 80cm
Private collection

Mario Pinton

Italy b.1919

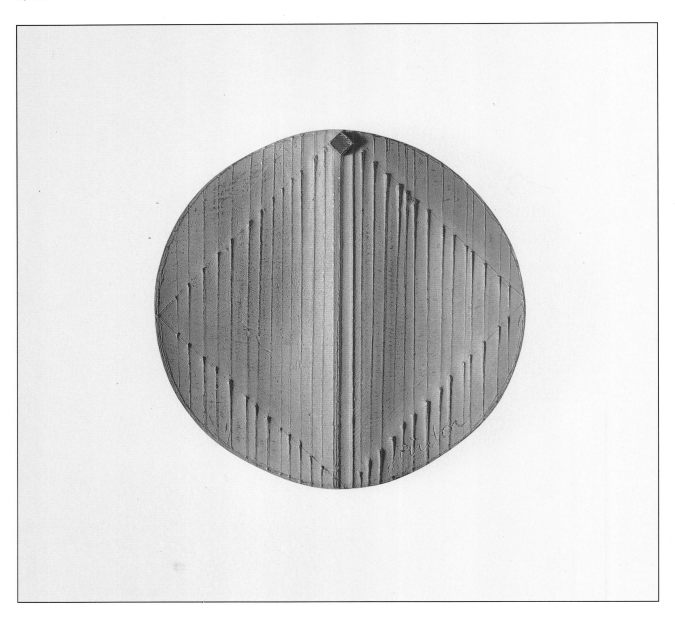

Pinton is an acknowledged master of contemporary
jewellery, and a formative influence on the significant
group of goldsmiths centred in Padua. Trained as a
goldsmith and sculptor, his works possess a relaxed
elegance of form which is founded on the confident
manipulation of his medium – gold – and an assured
apprehension as to the uses and purposes of jewellery.

Brooch 1986
18ct gold, ruby
4cm (diameter)
Private collection

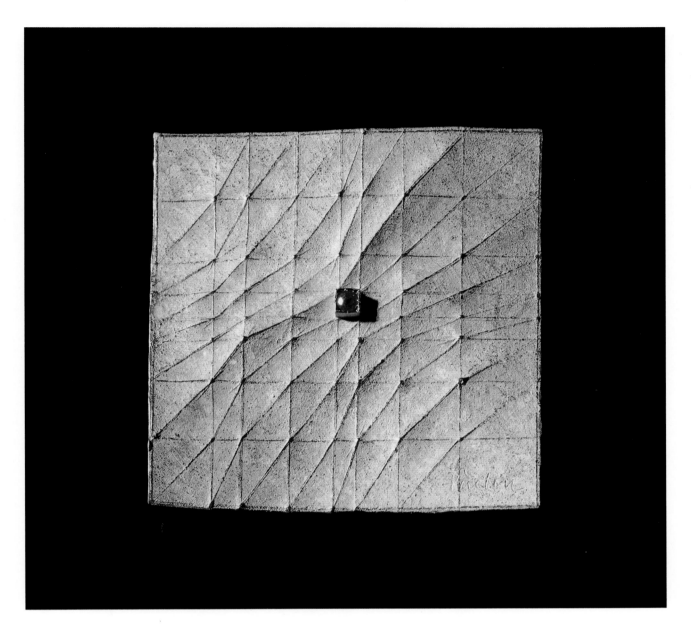

Brooch 1990
18ct gold, ruby
3.4 × 3.4cm
Museum für Kunst und Gewerbe, Hamburg

Ramón Puig Cuyas

Spain b.1953

In a way, Puig Cuyas' style and imagery is a personal conjunction of "isms": post-modernism, which legitimised an array of signs and symbols, and the new expressionism which, amongst other things, has endorsed a very free approach to metals. Metals can be teased or distressed into producing a wide range of expression, often by means which seem crude or casually disdainful of their "finer qualities". Here a sampling of that range portrays narrative pictorial schemes which are characteristically theatrical – like miniature stage sets.

La Porta/The Door
Brooch 1992
Alpaca (nickel silver), gold, wood
8.2 × 4.5cm
Private collection

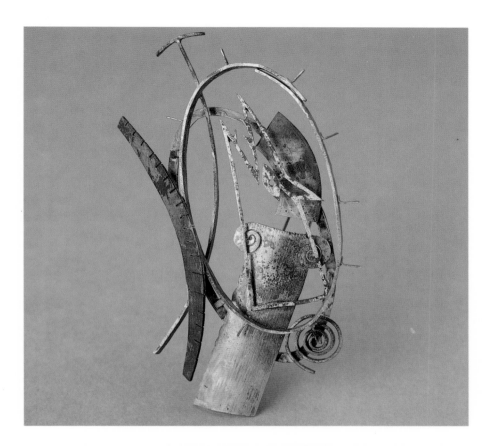

El Llop/The Wolf
Brooch 1992
Alpaca (nickel silver), gold
6.5 × 10cm
Private collection

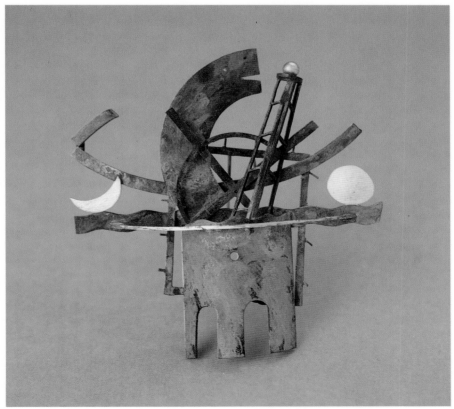

Un Día Quansevol/An Anyday Day
Brooch 1992
Alpaca (nickel silver), silver, gold
7.5 × 7.5cm
Private collection

Wolfgang Rahs

Austria b.1952

Certomlyk

Neckpiece 1990–92

Brass

27.5 × 20.5cm

Artist's collection

Kelermeskaja

Neckpiece 1990–93

Silver, tin

42 × 18cm

Artist's collection

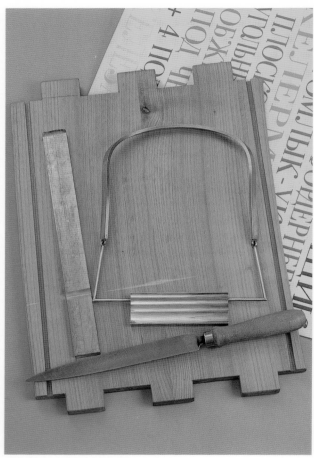

Rahs acts out a deeply felt sense of culture, history, place and location through his jewellery. This explores the intimate coexistence of things which come to be the way they are by association and inter-action rather than by design. His closely attentive drawing-out and manipulation of tractable, but otherwise "dead", materials, sets up subtle communications with the intelligence and sensuality of the living wearer.

Workbench Banquet

Shoulderpiece 1993

Silver, brass

64 × 24 × 15cm

Artist's collection

Workbench Banquet

Necklace 1993

Silver

41 × 17cm

Artist's collection

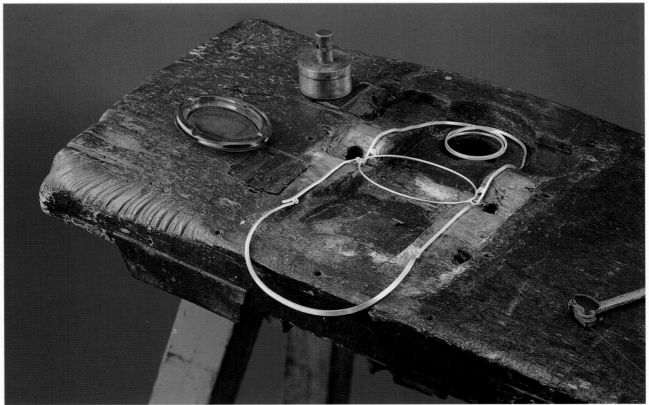

Wendy Ramshaw

UK b.1939

Ramshaw invented the ring-set and the ring-stand, both major innovative additions to the typology of jewellery, and the latter a significant contribution to any discussion of jewellery as autonomous object or "sculpture". A self-taught jeweller, her work is beautifully made, her approach compositional. Pieces full of incident accumulate from single elements. In spite of the influence of such painters as Klee and Kandinsky, she belongs firmly in the tradition of the decorative arts, where material, form, ornament and use are perfectly combined.

Transformer

Ring set on stand 1992

18ct yellow and white gold, 9ct red gold; nickel alloy

c. 16cm

Musée des Arts Décoratifs, Paris

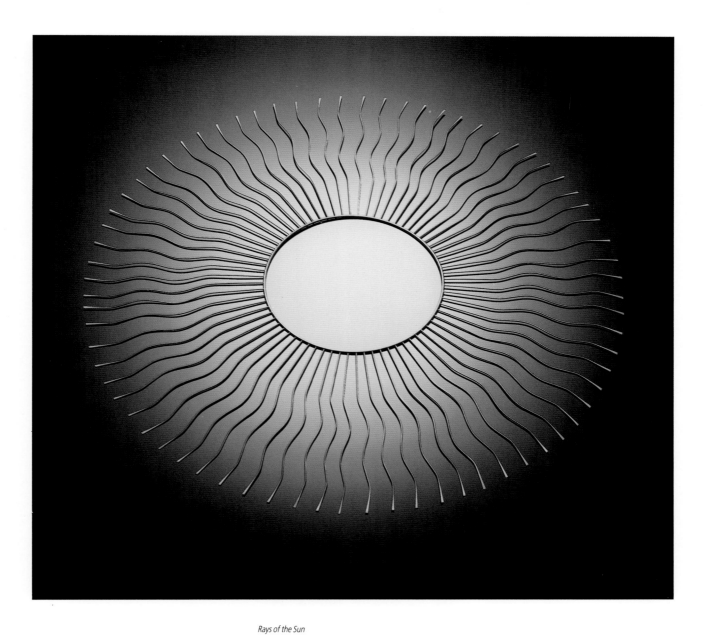

Rays of the Sun
Neckpiece 1989
Silver gilt
50cm (diameter)
Artist's collection

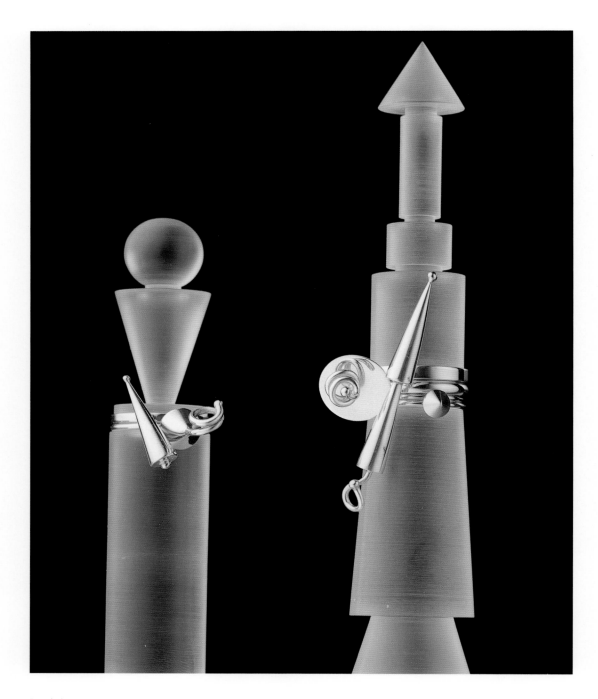

Transpiration
Rings on stands 1992
Silver, gold; acrylic
c. 15cm
Artist's collection

2 Brooches 1992
Oxidised silver
c. 15cm
Private collection

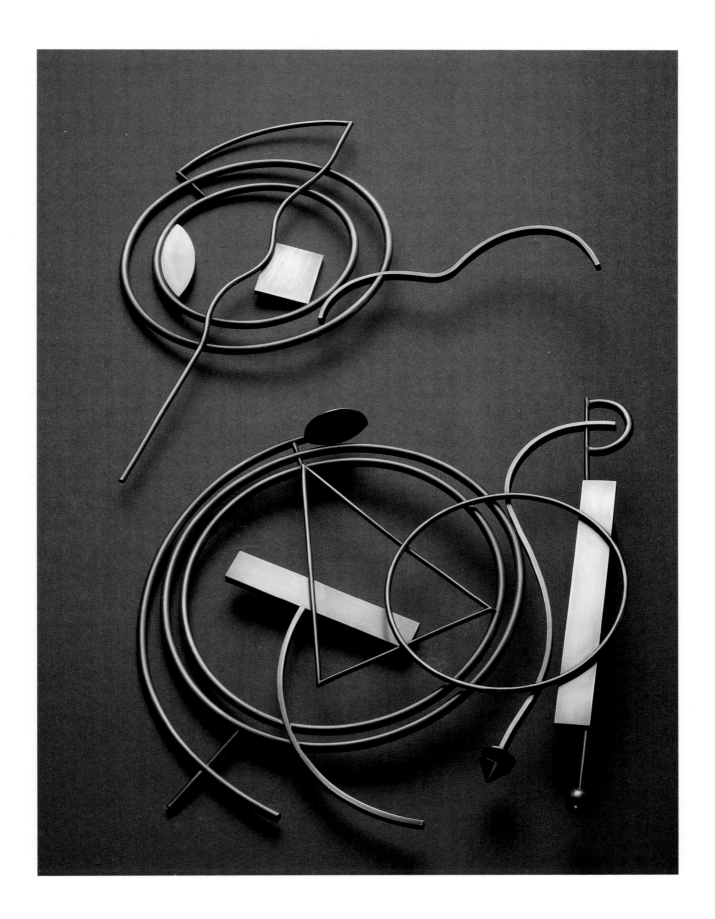

Gerd Rothmann

Germany b. 1941

Rothmann exploits the faithfulness of fine casting to make rich and complex images of flesh upon flesh, skin upon skin. Virtually no promontory, cleft or crevice of the body has escaped his attention, and the results make us acutely aware of the surfaces, interstices and mobility of our outer selves, at the final physical interface. Here, one may wear (all wrapped up in the erotic ambiguity of gold) an image of the sensation of self, or of the touch of another. It is in a way a rather simple idea, but played out with elegance and real artistry.

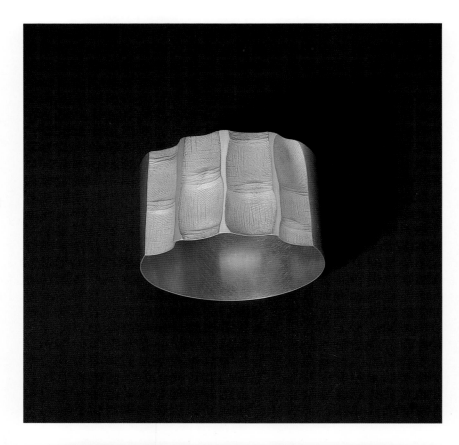

Vier-Finger-Armreif/Four finger bracelet
Bracelet 1992
18ct gold
6.8 × 4.3cm
Private collection

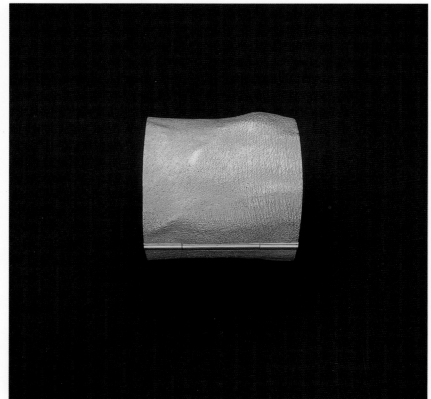

Von ihm für sie/From him for her
Bracelet 1990
18ct gold
5 × 6 × 5.5cm
Private collection

Wachskugeln flach gedrückt/Wax balls pressed flat
Necklace 1988
Gold
21cm (diameter)
Private collection

Siegelring/Signet ring
Ring 1987
18ct gold
1.3 × 2.2 × 2.6cm
Private collection

Philip Sajet

The Netherlands b.1953

Sajet has not fixed on a single subject matter or style for his work. Perhaps he is inclined to question contemporary conventions governing accepted good or appropriate design and content. As he says of his working process, "when one works, one waits for things to fall into place". This is not in itself an unusual perception. He wishes the imaginative process to remain receptive, uniformed, and his pieces possess a sort of modest intricacy which remains, however, very individual.

Thunder and Lightning
Neckpiece 1993
Steel, gold
29.5 × 21cm
Private collection

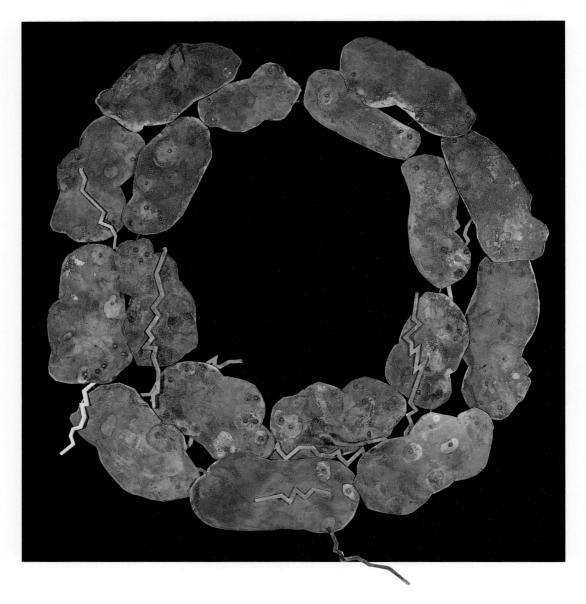

Byzantine Ring
Ring 1988
Gold, rock crystal, beads
5cm (height)
Private collection

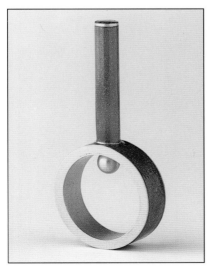

Der Chinesische Ring/The Chinese Ring
Ring 1990
Gold, enamel
5.5cm
Artist's collection

Flower Ring
Ring 1991
Gold, enamel, rubies
3.5cm (height)
Private collection

Marjorie Schick
USA b 1941

Collar 1993
Papier mâché, card, wood, paint
48 × 57 × 15cm
Artist's collection

Live Show
Collar 1992
Papier mâché, card, metal, wire, paint
51 × 60 × 23cm
Artist's collection

Wall Sculpture with Armlet
Armlet 1992
Papier mâché, card, metal, wire, paint
Sculpture: 43 × 64 × 11cm; armlet: 14 × 20 × 21cm
Private collection

Schick's earlier, more linear, but equally colourful, body
constructions were "discovered" by Europe in the eighties,
when they were found to be sympathetic with a non-
precious jewellery avant-garde of the time. It was soon
apparent that this was a chance meeting of interests, and
that she pursued an independent agenda. Her work
inhabits a cross-over area, between jewellery, sculpture
and clothing and is intrinsically "American" in its outgoing,
unfettered confidence. Her own phrase, "paintings to
wear", says it all.

Bernhard Schobinger

Switzerland b.1946

Schobinger stands very firmly for the right of a jewel function outside received methods and standards – whether of the academy or commerce. His oeuvre is diverse, concerning the materials as well as the subject matter of jewellery, and ranges from subversive to polemical in intention. His work makes a statement, has a point of view, and is driven by the opportunism of wit and intuition rather than the unfolding of an intellectual programme of design. The results can be powerful and often disturbing jewellery.

Holiday in Cambodia
Bracelet 1990
Silver
Private collection

Mit Licht gebohrter Diamant/Diamond d
Ring 1991
Gold, diamond
Private collection

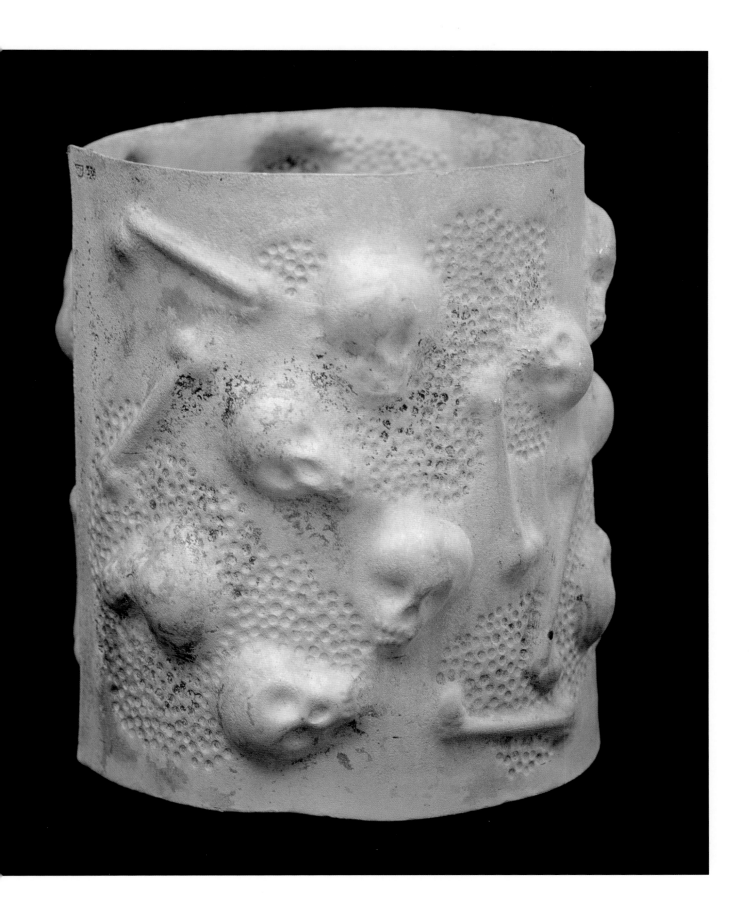

Paradiesgarten/Garden of paradise
Armband 1990
Gold
6.5cm (diameter); 9cm (height)
Private collection

Flaschenhalskette/Bottle necklace
Necklace 1990
Glass, cord
80cm
Private collection

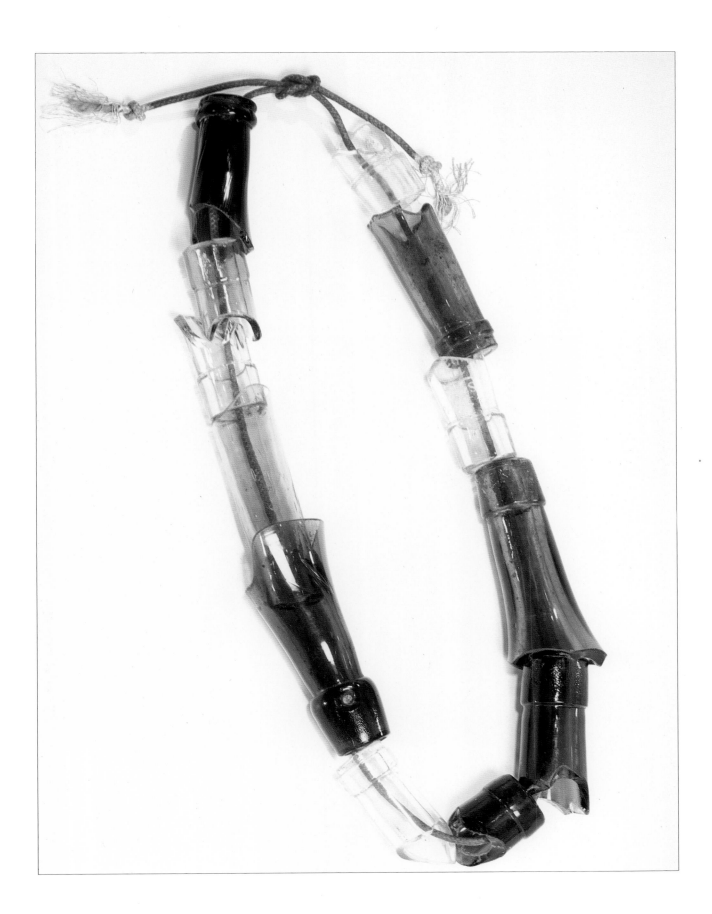

Deganit Schocken

Israel b.1947

Schocken's work is somehow bound up with the idea of
the dignity in remnants, certainly anti-design, and here
they are distributed across the body as if scattered across a
landscape, but found, located, marked and tied together.
On a mundane level, this topographical approach to
jewellery is about the attachment of brooches to clothing,
an issue pursued at schools in Jerusalem and London where
Schocken was a student in the 1970s. On the level of
meaning, however, this informal and touching
paraphernalia is strikingly metaphorical.

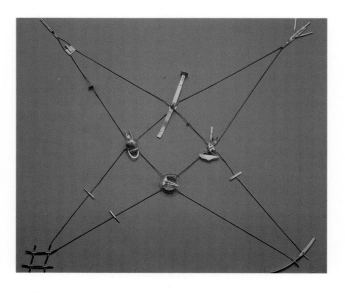

Signs of Personality
Body piece 1990
Silver, gold, stainless steel
90 × 90cm
Private collection

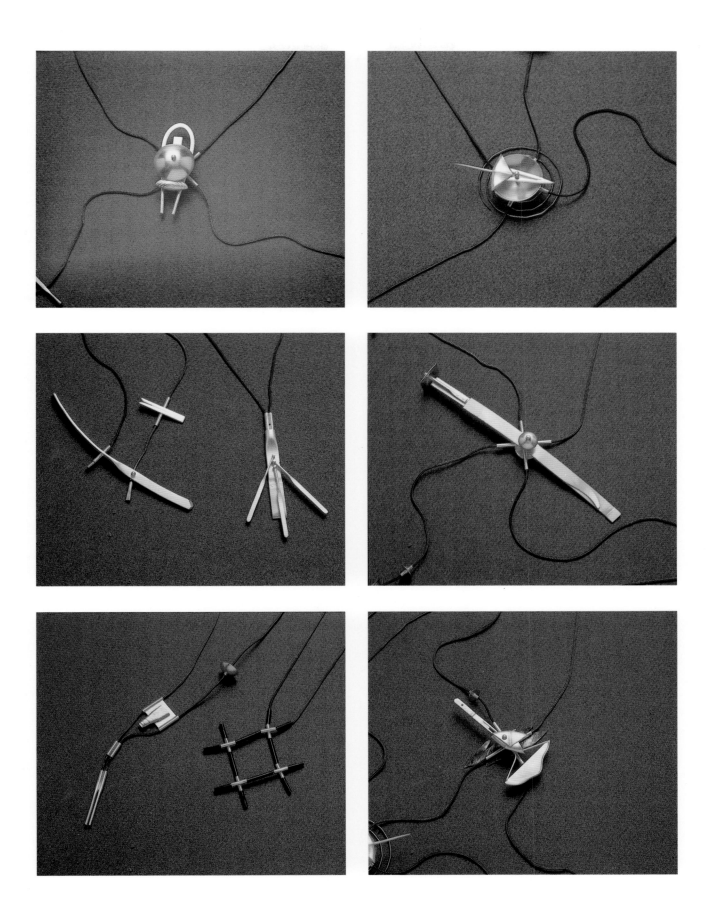

Robert Smit

The Netherlands b.1971

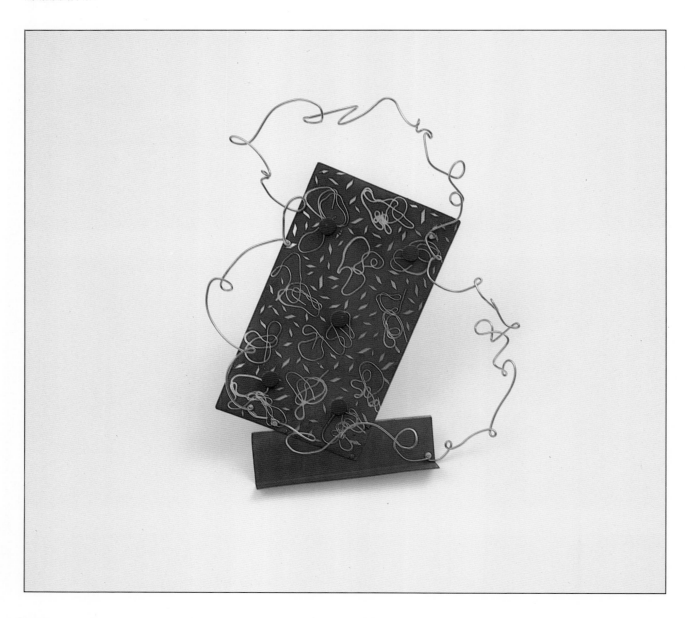

Bello – A Double Portrait

Brooch 1992

Gold, pearls, paint

10 × 13cm

Private collection

When Dutch jewellery reflected an ideological polarisation between precious and non-precious tendencies, Smit emerged as a leading activist for the former. In his own work of recent years he has, through the medium of jewellery, exploited processes and styles gathered from a compendium of expressionist fine art. His basic strategy is to treat his material – always high carat gold – as equivalent to the painter's canvas or the sculptor's steel, casually "improving" it. Although this apparent disregard for the material's conventional worth might be expected to devalue it, the trick, of course, is that it usually has the opposite effect.

Königin Bello/Queen Bello

Brooch 1992

Gold, pearls, paint

23 × 16.5cm

Private collection

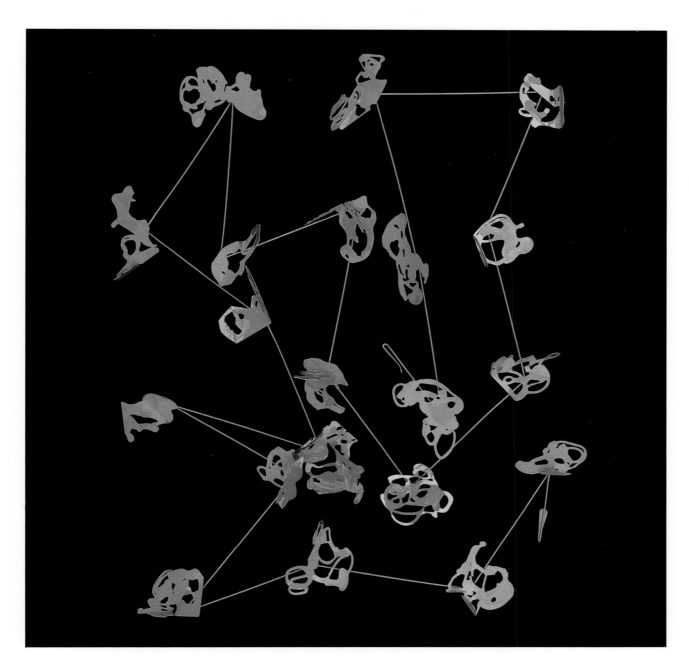

Chain 1991
Gold, paint
140cm
Private collection

Pendant 1991
Gold, paint
12.5 × 12.5cm
Private collection

Rachelle Thiewes
USA b.1952

Reflections of St Mary's
Necklace 1991
Silver, 18ct gold
68.5cm
Susan Davidoff collection

Thiewes, a professor of art in Texas, has developed jewels
which literally depend on the body. In necklaces of
exaggerated length, the pendant cluster hangs in the
pelvic region. The wearer's movement is transferred to the
necklace, setting it swinging and clinking. In presenting
her brooches against photographic prints, she goes beyond
factual description to create a silent ambiguity, but still the
overriding message is of sound and motion.

Silent Dance
Brooch 1992
Silver, black and white photograph
Photograph: 102 × 76 × 5cm; brooch: 36.5 × 15 × 1.2cm
Artist's collection

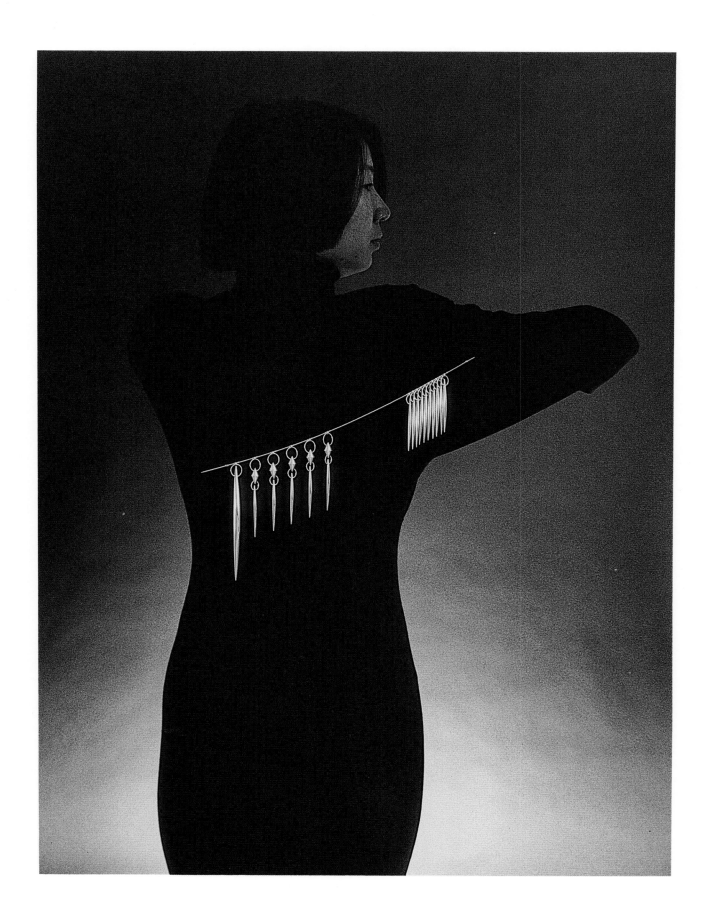

Reflections of St Mary's
Necklace 1991
Silver, 18ct gold, slate
66cm
Artist's collection

Silent Dance
Brooch 1992
Silver, black and white photograph
Photograph: 102 × 76 × 5cm; brooch: 36.5 × 15 × 1.2cm
Artist's collection

Detlef Thomas

Germany b.1959

Thomas was educated in Cologne and Munich. His work is characterised by complex but meandering constructions which are arboreal, as well as theatrical in their unconcern for rational form – baroque and operatic. In a way, what should be the external show has become the structural substance – like an exoskeleton – or the core has been eaten away. Concepts which could easily slide into prettiness project an uneasy sense of seduction and dissolution.

Neckpiece 1990

Silver

Artist's Collection

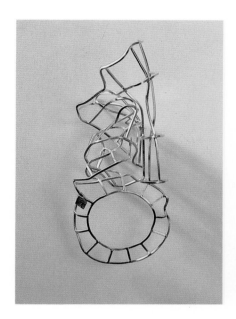

Ring 1992
18ct gold
6cm
Artist's collection

Ring 1993
18ct gold
5cm
Artist's collection

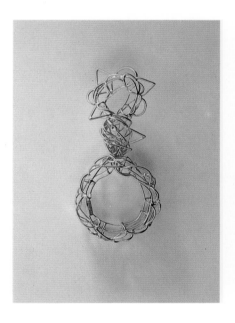

Ring 1992
18ct gold
6cm
Artist's collection

Ring 1992
18ct gold
6.5cm
Artist's collection

Andreas Treykorn

Germany b.1960

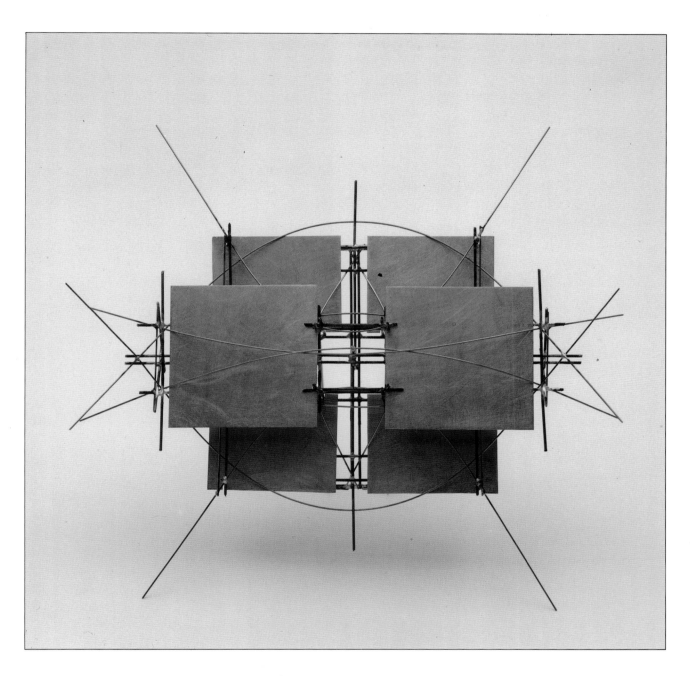

It seems appropriate that these images of enclosure, fragmentation and entrapment should have come from a Berliner. The delicacy and fastidiousness of the construction does not overshadow the expressive qualities of the junctions. Perhaps, for architects, "God is in the details", but, for jewellers, Truth is at the junctions.

Neckpiece 1992
Silver mesh
45 × 18cm
Vestlandske Kunstindustri Museum, Bergen, Norway

Brooch 1993
Tempered steel, brass
3 × 9 × 12cm
Private collection

Tone Vigeland
Norway b.1938

Cap 1992
Silver
22.6 × 12.8cm
Private collection

Cap (detail) 1992

Cap 1992
Silver
22 × 21.5cm
Kunstindustri Museet, Oslo, Norway

Vigeland's weighty jewellery is based upon experiments in chainmail. The ebb and flow of constant adjustment as many pieces move with the body is central to this highly developed aesthetic, as is the simplicity and uniformity of shape which the chainmail technique allows. This stringent, principled and sombre work, with its undisguised evocation of a northern warrior culture is, however, quickly discovered to be very beautiful and easy to wear by its many admirers and collectors.

Neckpiece 1992
Silver
45 × 18 cm
Vestlandske Kunstindustrie Museum, Bergen

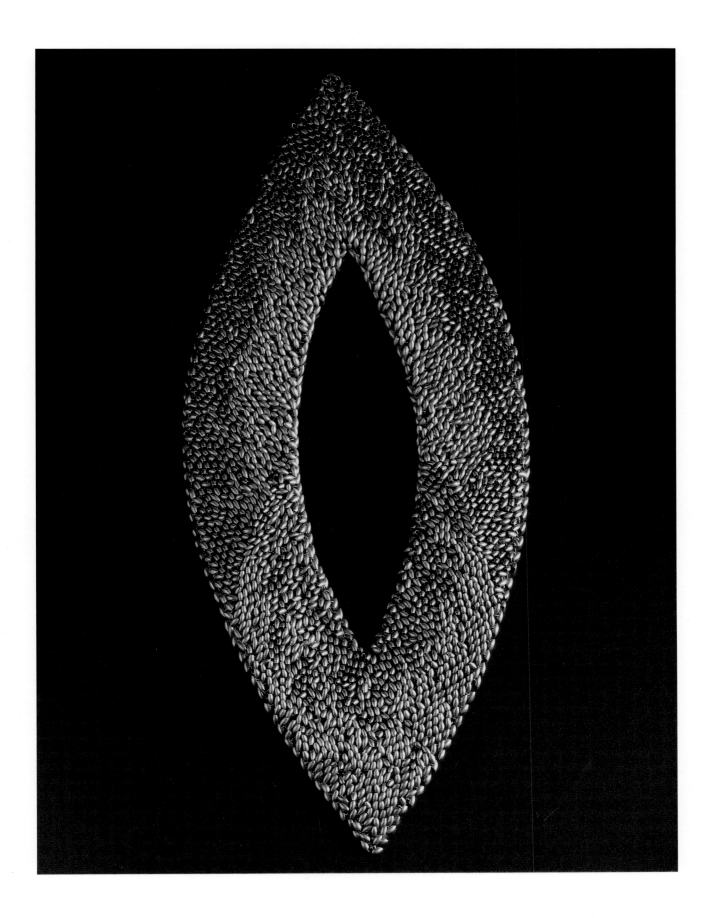

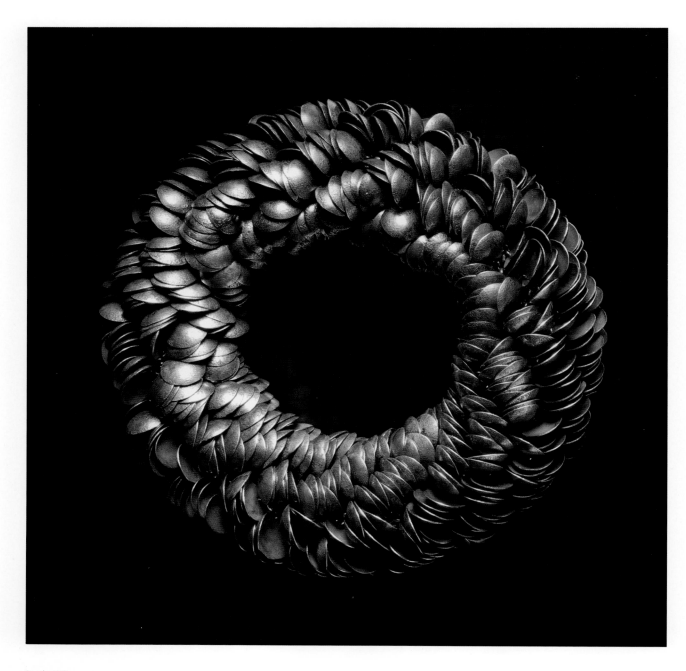

Bracelet 1992
Silver mesh
11.5cm (diameter)
Vestlandske Kunstindustri Museum, Bergen, Norway

Neckpiece 1992
Silver
40 × 19cm
Nordenfjeldske Kunstindustri Museum, Trondheim, Norway

Neckpiece 1992
Silver
35 × 26cm
Private collection

Graziano Visintin

Italy b.1954

Visintin is fascinated by narrow facets and minimal volumes. He wraps his facets around essentially linear forms, opening them out and closing them down, to give and take dimension as the line angles around from point to point. In the circular neckpiece, a similar technique is used. There are some risks in using such a simple, generic form – and it does not offer the ready dynamics of something angular or assembled – but the outcome is individual and lyrical, is attenuated delicacy finely tuned.

Necklace 1990
18ct gold
22cm (diameter)
Private collection

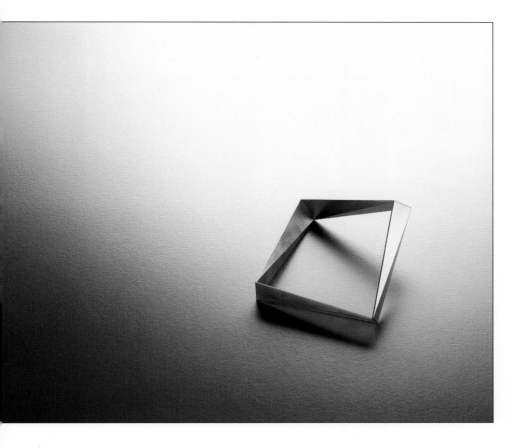

Bracelet 1990
18ct gold
7 × 7 × 1.2cm
Private collection

Necklace 1992
18ct gold
24cm (diameter)
Private collection

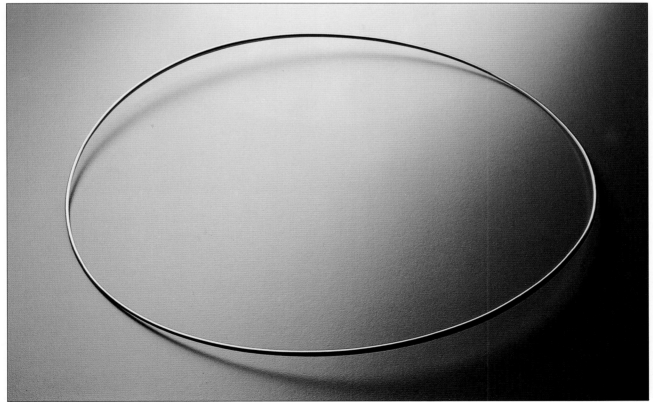

David Watkins

UK b.1940

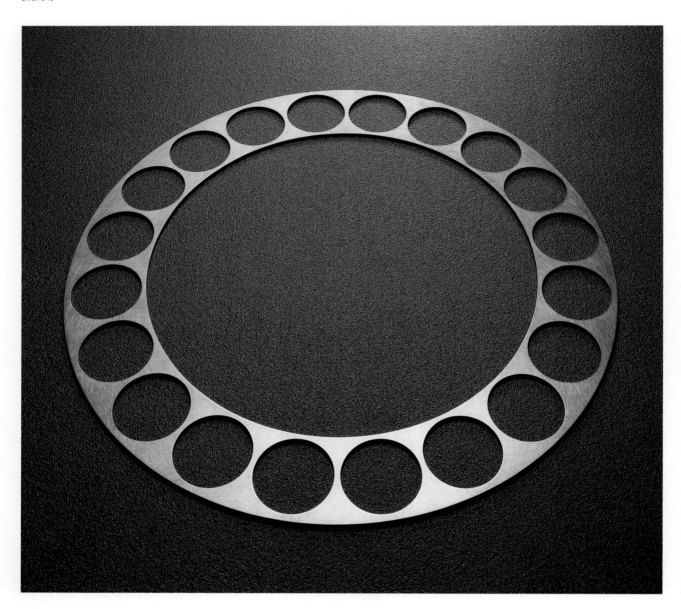

Torus 280 (B2)
Neckpiece 1989
Gilded brass
28cm
Private collection

Surf 1
Brooch 1990
Silver
15 × 2cm
Private collection

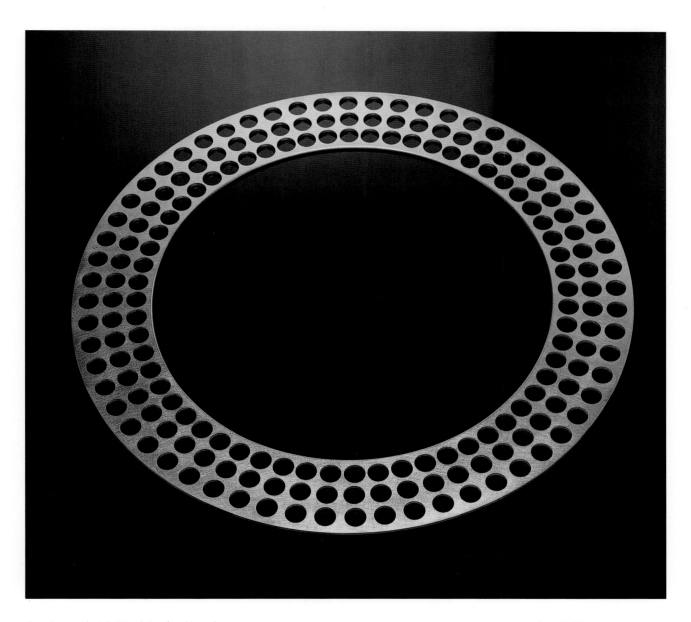

These pieces are about the interrelation of precision and image, technology and romance the new and archaic, and especially – in the context of a "modern" jewellery – of the tensions between form and ornament. They are made by varying combinations of machine and hand. They are quite ordered, in essence symmetrical, seeking a simple and cogent expression of an idea. All this, however, is bound up with and conditional upon their status as objects to be worn.

Torus 280 (B1)
Neckpiece 1989
Gilded brass
28cm
Museum für Kunst und Gewerbe, Hamburg

Leaf Pin 1
Brooch 1993
Gold
11 × 8.5cm
Private collection

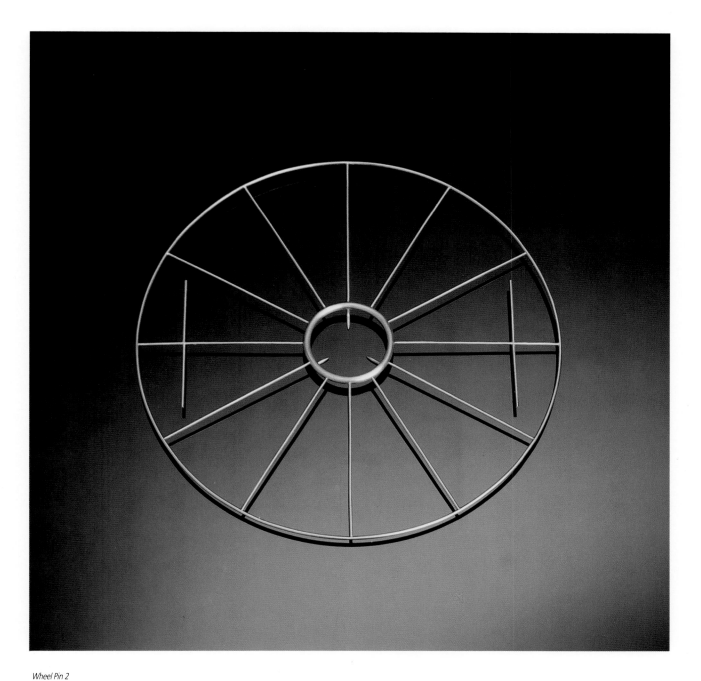

Wheel Pin 2
Brooch 1993
Gold
11cm
Private collection

Anette Wohlleber

Germany b.1962

Some jewellery primarily addresses the world of the imagination. That it might be worn seems incidental to its purposes. Wohlleber evokes dreams and remembrances – perhaps from childhood – with the quality of fairy tales. Our responses must remain uncertain. The pieces are saved from a threatened sentimentality by fragmentation, decay, and physicality. The phenomena of metal techniques can lend themselves very well to this aesthetic, and Wohlleber exploits them with skill.

Windmühle/Windmill
Brooch 1991
Oxidised silver
7.6 × 12 × 1.5cm
Private collection

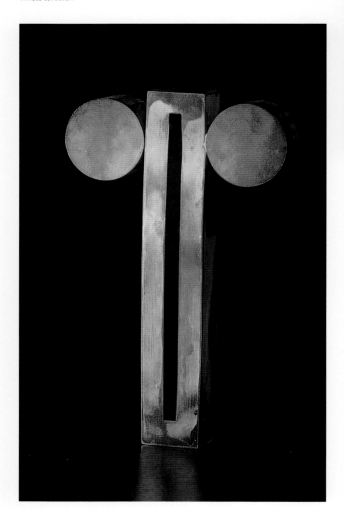

Hochofen/Blast-furnace
Brooch 1991
Oxidised silver, gold leaf
7 × 10 × 1.8cm
Private collection

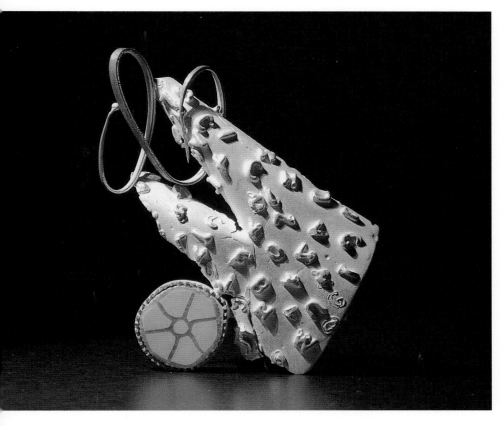

Nudelwagen/Noodlecar
Brooch 1991
Silver, polyester, noodle
10.5 × 7 × 1cm
Private collection

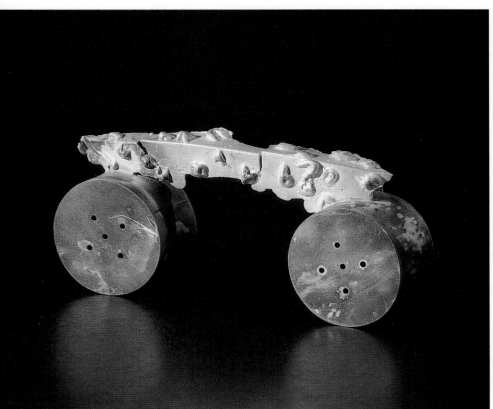

Wagen/Car
Brooch 1991
Oxidised silver
9 × 4 × 2cm
Private collection

Irmgard Zeitler

Germany b.1957

Rose Ball
Pendant 1992
18ct gold, rock crystal, spinel
5.3 × 2.5cm
Private collection

Berry
Pendant 1990
18/22ct gold, acrylic, tourmaline
6 × 3.2cm
Private collection

Zeitler's characteristically jagged abstractions of fruit and flowers also carry in their stylised ornamentation more than a hint of baroque. They are certainly secular – almost "fashionable" – in intention, but "devotional" in their attention to the quality of making, and further enriched by association with the ornament of sacred places and ritual objects. This intensity and ambiguity, in a contemporary context, in effect contributes to their singularity.

Cactus Flowers
Ear piece 1990
22ct gold, silver, acrylic
12 × 4cm
Private collection

Othmar Zschaler

Switzerland b. 1930

Zschaler animates the surface of his gold jewellery with great skill. It carries a sense of landscape intensely experienced, but not imitated. The material fixes itself as being torn from sheet metal and yet also suggests a geological event. The image of a mountain landscape – distant twisted strata and shards of rock – is persuasive in itself, but the underlying coherence of such associations is authenticated by the literal truth that gold and precious stones must be found amongst rocks.

Bracelet 1992
18ct gold
4.2 × 6cm
Private collection

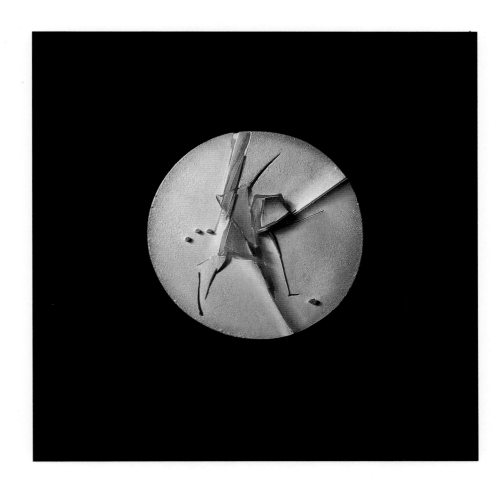

Brooch 1992
18ct gold
5cm (diameter)
Private collection

IMAGE

There is a tradition of making jewellery or small objects that are meant to be admired for their own sakes. We are invited to enjoy their beauty, to be diverted by their intricacy, to interpret their symbolism, to discover and share in the knowledge of their secret workings, quite apart from any connection with the body. In this territory, jewellery begins to merge with *objet d'art*. Such pieces predominantly engage the mind and the moment.

Another tradition is talismanic: objects are intended to be handled more than worn, to be treasured intimately and enjoyed for their haptic qualities, to be worn only — if at all — in a contingent way, perhaps casually attached as on a chain. When they are openly worn, on display, there is a sense in which the private is brought out into the public domain — a subtle disclosure of self. This work predominantly engages the senses and remembrances.

Near their extremes, neither of these traditions or attitudes would suggest the priority of wearing the jewellery. But precisely what distinguishes jewellery from all other arts is its particular relationship to the human body — this is of the essence, its unique gift and its special frame of reference. In the end, every element of its thought and practice, however remote, is driven by that linkage.

Compared with the commercial world, where the makers and sellers of jewellery are quick to use photography to project an ideal, co-ordinated image for the piece and the wearer, artist jewellers are often more reticent. Many will be reluctant to associate their jewellery with any single "look" or type, and do not see it as their function to suggest how, by whom, or in what conditions their work should be used. The jewellery is given a life of its own, qualities which are to be discovered and enjoyed by anyone who is receptive to them; it should not become hostage to the conceptual limitations of a constructed image. Others will be interested to follow their work as it extends into the realm of wearing and using, to explore and record its consequent conceptual and creative possibilities — its transformed and transforming potential in the world. A significant number will want to experience and test

their assumptions and conceptions "in the round", grounded in that reality, engaging the inanimate with the animate. In terms of photographic images, there are risks in all this. Unless there is some clear guiding intention, the results of on-the-body photography can all too easily slip into the merely glamorous or simply banal. The first will threaten to devalue the jewellery, the second to neutralise the whole endeavour.

At best, images of jewellery being worn will reveal some other, perhaps unexpected dimension of the work, or communicate a more acute understanding of its meanings and potential beyond the simply obvious. It is possible, contrary to reservations about inhibiting stereotypes, that the work will in fact be set free, released into the world, in ways which cannot be appreciated through a still-life or show case.

This section sets out to compare some of the ways contemporary jewellers will explore and communicate their jewellery, and their feelings and ideas *about* jewellery, through photographs of it being worn. In more than one sense of the word, it is a selection of "attitudes".

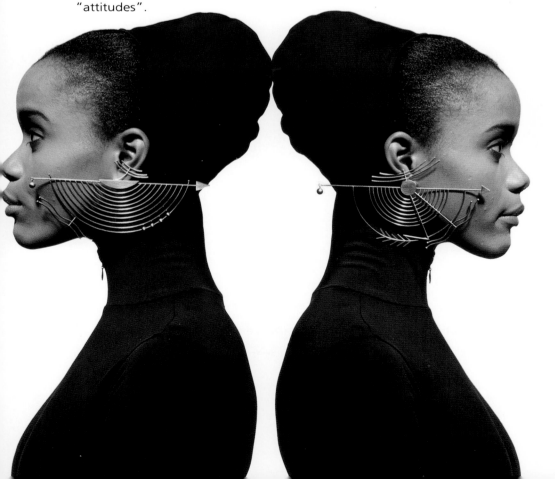

Petra Hartman

Heart with Teardrop

1992

Svatopluk Kasaly
Necklace
1991

 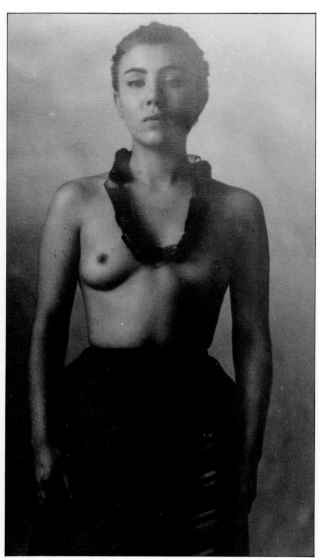

Bernhard Schobinger

Sonia with Rusted Cross/Sonja mit Sägenkreuz

Sonia with Bottle Neckpiece/Sonja mit Flaschenhalskette

Bruce Metcalf

Wood Pin #69

1991

Fritz Maierhofer
Ring #4

Jacomȳn van der Donk

Ring #3A
1993

Ring #1A
1991

Ring #4A
1993

Gijs Bakker

Nipple

1991

The Tongue

1989

Gerd Rothmann

Wachskugeln flach gedrükt/Wax balls pressed flat

1988

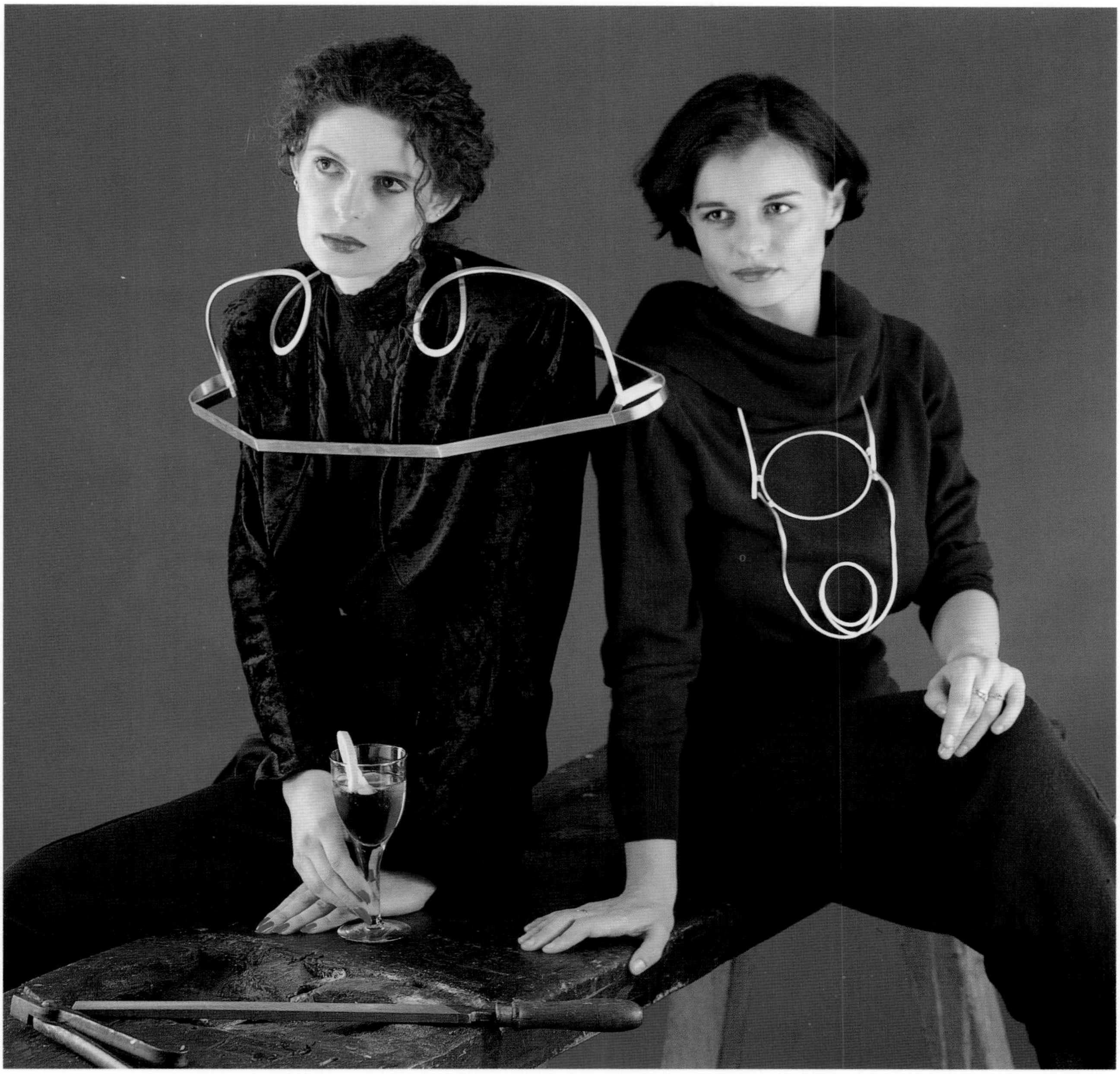

Wolfgang Rahs

Workbench Banquet

1993

Carlier Makigawa
Brooch
1991

Ulrike Bahrs

Egg, Wool and Metal
1990

Egg, Wool and Metal 9
1990

 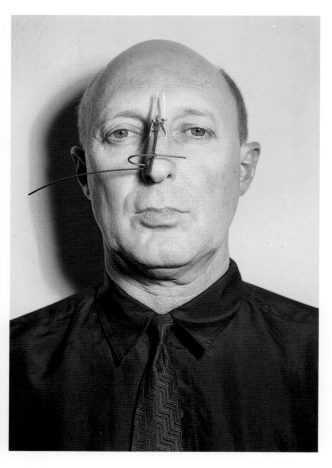

Susan Cohn

Cosmetic Manipulations – Chin
1992

Cosmetic Manipulations – Nose
1992

Peter Chang
Bracelets
1987

Wendy Ramshaw

Catherine Wheel

1990

Petra Hartman

Giant Necklace

1992

Tone Vigeland

Silver Cap 22
1992

Silver Cap 33
1992

Wendy Ramshaw

Earrings for Woman with Large Profile

1989

Yasuki Hiramatsu
Crown
1991

Lisa Gralnick
Bracelet
1987

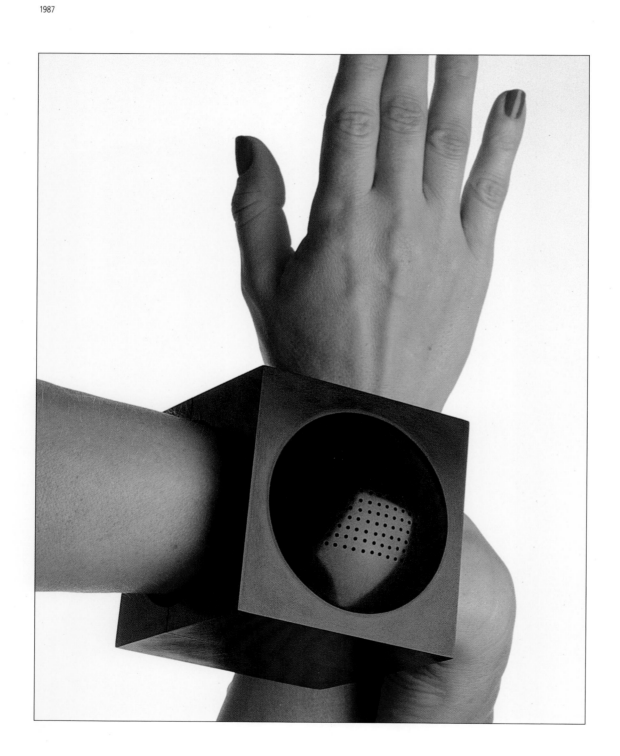

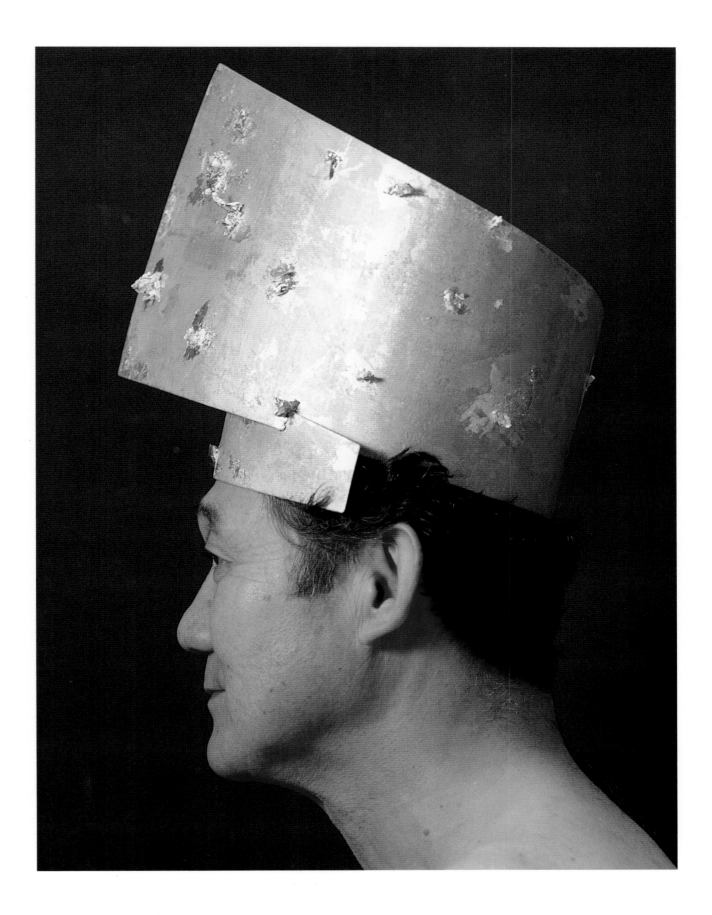

Gilles Jonemann

David Watkins

Torus 280 (B3)

1990

Artist Profiles

Gijs Bakker

Netherlands 1942

Senior Lecturer at AIVE (Man and Living Department)

STUDIES Instituut voor Kunstnijverheidsonderwijs (Gerrit Rietveld
Academie), Amsterdam, Netherlands (1959–62); Konstfack
Skolan, Stockholm, Sweden (1962–3)

AWARDS Françoise van den Bosch prize for jewellery design (1988)

RECENT EXHIBITIONS Galerie Ra, Amsterdam (1986, 1989,
1991); Helen Williams Drutt, New York, USA (1989);
Retrospectif, Centraal Museum, Utrecht, Netherlands (1989);
Kunstrai, Amsterdam (1989); Helen Williams Drutt, Philadelphia,
USA (1991)

WORKS IN PUBLIC COLLECTIONS Stedelijk Museum, Amsterdam,
Netherlands; Museum Boymans van Beuningen, Rotterdam,
Netherlands; Cleveland County Museum, Middlesbrough, UK;
Power House Museum, Sydney, Australia; National Museum of
Modern Art, Kyoto, Japan; Cooper Hewitt Museum, New York

James Bennett

USA 1948

Professor of Art, State University of New York, USA

STUDIES State University of New York; USA; University of
Georgia, Athens, USA

AWARDS National Endowment for the Arts, 1973, 1979, 1988

RECENT EXHIBITIONS CDK Gallery, New York, USA (1989);
Schneider Gallery, Chicago, USA (1990); Clark Gallery Boston,
USA (1991); Galerie Jocelyne Gobeil, Montreal, Canada (1992);
"Facet I", International Biennale, Rotterdam, Netherlands (1993)

Giampaolo Babetto

Italy 1947

STUDIES Istituto d'Arte Pietro Selvatico, Padua, Italy (1979–80);
Accademia di Belle Arti, Venezia, Italy

AWARDS Grand Prix, Japan (1983)

RECENT EXHIBITIONS Provinciaal Museum Voor Moderne Kunst,
Ostend, Belgium (1989); Musée d'Art Moderne et
Contemporaine, Nice, France (1992); Kunstverein, Düsseldorf,
Germany (1992); Museum für Kunst und Gewerbe, Hamburg,
Germany (1993)

WORKS IN PUBLIC COLLECTIONS Victoria & Albert Museum,
London, UK; Musée des Arts Décoratifs, Paris, France; Musée
d'Art Moderne, Nice, France; Museum für Kunst und
Gewerbe, Hamburg, Germany; Schmuckmuseum, Pforzheim,
Germany; Art Gallery of Western Australia, Perth, Australia

Ulrike Bahrs

Germany 1944

STUDIES Akademie der Bildenden Künste, Munich, Germany

RECENT EXHIBITIONS "Arts and Crafts of Germany", Japan,
Singapore, China (1985); Electrum Gallery, London, UK (1985);
"Art and the Invisible Reality" (symposium), New York, USA
(1989); Galerie der Laden, Frankfurt, Germany (1992)

WORKS IN PUBLIC COLLECTIONS Museum für Kunst und
Gewerbe, Hamburg, Germany; Schmuckmuseum, Pforzheim,
Germany; Landes Museum, Schleswig, Germany

WORKS IN PUBLIC COLLECTIONS American Craft Museum, New
York, USA; Royal College of Art, London, UK; National Museum
of American Art, Renwick Gallery, New Haven, USA;
Kunstindustrimuseum, Trondheim, Norway; Arkansas Museum
of Decorative Arts, Little Rock, Arkansas, USA

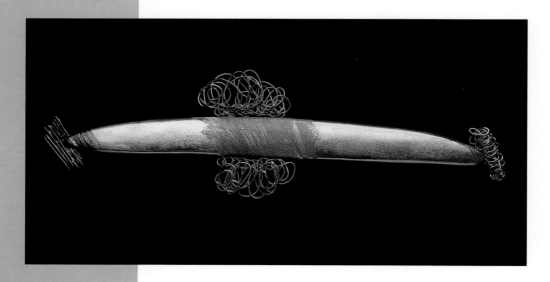

Liv Blåvarp

Norway   1956

STUDIES State College of Art and Design, Oslo, Norway
(1979–83); Royal College of Art, London, UK (1983–4)

RECENT EXHIBITIONS "Scandinavia Today", Tokyo, Japan and
New York, USA (1987); Künstnerforbündet, Oslo (1988);
"Nordform", Malmö, Sweden (1990); Gallery RAM, Oslo (1991);
"Norwegian Wood" (touring in Europe, 1991) .

WORKS IN PUBLIC COLLECTIONS Museums of Applied Art, Oslo,
Trondheim and Bergen, Norway; Museum of Applied Art,
Copenhagen, Denmark; Røhsska Museum, Gothenburg,
Sweden; Cooper Hewitt Museum, New York, USA

Onno Boekhoudt

Netherlands   1944

Jeweller and Sculptor

Visiting tutor, Royal College of Art, London

STUDIES Vakschool, Schoonhoven, Netherlands (1963–6);
Academie Artibus, Utrecht, Netherlands (1963–6); Staatliche
Kunst und Werkschule, Pforzheim, Germany (1966–8)

RECENT EXHIBITIONS Galerie Ra, Amsterdam, Netherlands
(1987, 1991); Galerie Nouvelles Images, The Hague, Netherlands
(1987); Studio Ton Berends, The Hague, Netherlands (1990,
1993); Galerie No, Lausanne, Switzerland (1991); Gallery YU,
Tokyo Japan (1994)

WORKS IN PUBLIC COLLECTIONS Gemeente Museum, Arnhem,
Netherlands; Museum het Kruithuis, 'sHertogenbosch,
Netherlands; Power House Museum, Sydney, Australia

Rudolf Bott

Germany   1956

STUDIES Zeichenakademie, Hanau, Germany (1979–80)

AWARDS Frankfurt Herbstmesse (1992)

RECENT EXHIBITIONS Rezac Gallery, Chicago, USA (1988);
"Europäisches Kunsthandwerk 1991", Stuttgart, Germany
(1991); Schmuck und Gerät, Schloss Wertingen, Germany
(1991); Galerie Treykorn, Berlin, Germany (1992)

WORKS IN PUBLIC COLLECTIONS Stadtmuseum, Munich,
Germany

Joaquim Capdevila

Spain   1944

STUDIES Escola Massana, Barcelona, Spain (1958–64); Atelier
Lacambra, Paris, France (1965–6)

AWARDS Gold Medals, Bavarian State Exhibitions (1967, 1968);
Internationales Kunsthanwerk, Stuttgart (1969); "Mostra
d'Artesania d'Avantguarda", Barcelona (1980)

RECENT EXHIBITIONS Galerie am Graben, Vienna, Austria
(1986); "Joieria Europa Contemporània", Barcelona, Spain
(1987); "Design in Catalonia" (touring Milan, Berlin, Stuttgart,
Stockholm, Nagoya, New York, 1989–90); 3rd Triennale du
Bijou, Musée des Arts Décoratifs, Paris, France (1992); Facet I,
Kunsthal, Rotterdam, Netherlands (1993)

WORKS IN PUBLIC COLLECTIONS Schmuckmuseum, Pforzheim,
Germany

Anton Cepka

Slovakia   1936

Jeweller and Sculptor; Professor of Metalwork, Academy of Fine
Arts, Bratislava.

STUDIES Secondary School of Applied Arts, Bratislava; Academy
of Fine Arts, Prague

AWARDS Bavaria Prize, Munich, 1964; The Golden Ring, Hanau,
1990

RECENT EXHIBITIONS Galerie am Graben, Vienna (1978, 1986);
Galerie Lousie Smit, Amsterdam, Netherlands (1987);
Goldschmiedehaus, Hanau (1989); Galerie Tiller, Vienna (1991)

WORKS IN PUBLIC COLLECTIONS Galerie Albertstrasse, Graz,
Austria; National Gallery, Melbourne, Australia; Galerie am
Graben, Vienna, Austria; Schmuckmuseum, Pforzheim,
Germany; Museum für Glas und Bijouterie, Jablonec, Czech
Republic

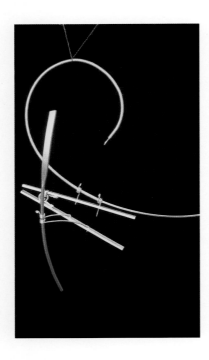

Peter Chang

UK   1944

Maker and designer of jewellery and tableware

STUDIES Liverpool College of Art, UK (1962–6); Slade School of Fine Art, London, UK (1968–71)

RECENT EXHIBITIONS Galerie Ra, Amsterdam, Netherlands (1988, 1990); Ornamenta 1, Pforzheim, Germany (1989); Helen Williams Drutt, New York, USA (1990); New Art Forms, Navy Pier, Chicago, USA (1990); Helen Williams Drutt, Philadelphia, USA (1992)

WORKS IN PUBLIC COLLECTIONS Crafts Council, London, UK; National Museum of Scotland, Edinburgh, UK; Montreal Museum of Decorative Art, Montreal, Canada; Victoria & Albert Museum, London; British Council Collection, Prague, Czech Republic

Susan Cohn

Australia   1952

Director of Workshop 3000, Melbourne, Australia

STUDIES Royal Melbourne Institute of Technology, Victoria, Australia (1980–6)

RECENT EXHIBITIONS Contemporary Jewellery Gallery, Sydney, Australia (1988); Seibu Loft Gallery, Shibuya, Tokyo, Japan (1989); " . . . and does it work?", City Gallery, Melbourne, Australia (1989); "Cosmetic Manipulations", City Gallery, Melbourne, Australia (1992); "Design Visions" Art Gallery of Western Australia, Perth (1992)

WORKS IN PUBLIC COLLECTIONS Australian National Gallery; Art Gallery of Victoria; Art Gallery of Western Australia; Power House Museum of Applied Arts and Sciences; Queen Victoria Museum and Art Gallery, Launceston, Australia

Cynthia Cousens

UK   1956

Part-time lecturer, Royal College of Art, London, UK

STUDIES Loughborough College of Art, UK (1975–8); Royal College of Art, London (1979–82)

RECENT EXHIBITIONS Victoria & Albert Museum, London, UK (1988); British Design, Mitsukoshi, Tokyo, Japan (1990); Scottish Gallery (1992); City Art Gallery, Leeds, UK (1992); Noblesse Oblique, Lausanne, Switzerland (1993)

WORKS IN PUBLIC COLLECTIONS Crafts Council, London; British Council, London; Southeast Arts, Hove Museum, UK; Shipley Collection, Gateshead, UK; Worshipful Company of Goldsmith's, London

Lam de Wolf

Netherlands   1949

STUDIES Gerrit Rietveld Academie le Amsterdam (1978–1981)

RECENT EXHIBITIONS Rietveld Academie, Amsterdam (1981); Het kruithuis, Holland (1982); Het Kapehuis, Holland (1982); Kunstmanifestatie, Holland (1982); Aspects, England (1983); Akut, Germany (1984)

Georg Dobler

Germany   1952

STUDIES Berufsfachschule für Goldschmiede, Pforzheim, Germany

RECENT EXHIBITIONS Galerie Ra, Amsterdam, Netherlands (1982, 1986, 1991); Galerie V & V, Vienna, Austria (1983, 1987, 1992); Galerie Spektrum, MUNICH, Germany (1987, 1992); Werkstattgalerie, Berlin, Germany (1984, 1988, 1991)

WORKS IN PUBLIC COLLECTIONS Stedelijk Museum, Amsterdam; Schmuckmuseum, Pforzheim; National Museum of Modern Art, Kyoto, Japan; Museum für Angewandte Kunst, Vienna, Austria; Kunstegewerbemuseum, Berlin, Germany; Gallery of Western Australia, Perth

Xavier Domenech

Spain 1960

Lecturer at Escola Massana, Barcelona (Jewellery Department)

STUDIES Escola Massana, Barcelona (1984–8)

AWARDS Premio Internacional Massana de Joyeria (1989)

RECENT EXHIBITIONS Galerie Hipotesi, Barcelona (1987); Galerie Montiel, Pamplona, Spain (1988); Galerie GU, Barcelona (1988); Contacto Directo Galeria, Lisbon, Portugal (1990); "Hola Barcelona", Galerie Jocelyne Gobeil, Montreal, Canada (1990)

WORKS IN PUBLIC COLLECTIONS Scottish Museum, Edinburgh, UK

Jacomyn van der Donk

Netherlands 1963

STUDIES Gerrit Rietveld Academie, Amsterdam, Netherlands (1986–91)

RECENT EXHIBITIONS "Jewellery as object –object as jewellery", Netherlands (1991); Facet I, Kunsthal, Rotterdam, Netherlands (1993); Galerie Louise Smit, Amsterdam (1992, 1993)

WORKS IN PUBLIC COLLECTIONS Stedelijk Museum, Amsterdam, Netherlands; Arnhem Museum, Netherlands

Arline M. Fish

USA 1931

Professor of Art, San Diego State University, California, USA

STUDIES Skidmore College, New York (1952); University of Illinois (1954); Kunsthaandvaerkerskolen, Copenhagen, Denmark (1956–7)

RECENT EXHIBITIONS Tendenzen, Schmuckmuseum, Pforzheim, Germany (1973, 1977); "Schmuck International", Vienna, Austria (1980); "International Jewellery", Tokyo, Japan (1983, 1986); Museum of Fine Arts, Montevideo, USA (1989)

WORKS IN PUBLIC COLLECTIONS American Craft Museum, New York, USA; National Museum of American Art, Renwick Gallery, New Haven, USA; Schmuckmuseum, Pforzheim, Germany; Victoria & Albert Museum, London, UK; Vatican Museum, Rome

Gerda Flöckinger

UK 1927

STUDIES St Martin's School of Art, London, UK; Central School of Arts and Crafts, London, UK

RECENT EXHIBITIONS "Schmuck International 1900–1980", Künstlerhaus, Vienna, Austria (1980); City of Bristol Museum and Art Gallery, UK (1981); Ornmenta 1, Pforzheim, Germany (1989)

WORKS IN PUBLIC COLLECTIONS Schmuckmuseum, Pforzheim, Germnay; Worshipful Company of Gooldsmith's, London, UK; Victoria & Albert Museum, London, UK; Crafts Council, London, UK; Royal Museum of Scotland, Edinburgh, UK

Lisa Gralnick

USA 1956

Head of Metals Department, Parsons School of Design, New York City, USA

STUDIES Kent State University, Ohio (1977); State University of New York, USA (1980)

RECENT EXHIBITIONS Gallery Vo, Washington DC, USA (1987); Galerie Ra, Amsterdam, Netherlands (1988); CDK Gallery, New York, USA (1989); Susan Cummins, Mill Valley, California, USA (1990); Jewelerswerk Galerie, Washington DC, USA (1991)

WORKS IN PUBLIC COLLECTIONS Stedelijk Museum, Amsterdam, Netherlands; American Craft Museum, New York, USA; Schenectady Museum, New York, USA

William Harper

USA   1944

Freelance artist

STUDIES Western Reserve University Cleveland, Ohio, USA (1967); Cleveland Institute of Art, USA (1967)

RECENT EXHIBITIONS "The Eloquent Objects" (touring, 1987–9); Victoria & Albert Museum, London, UK (1990); "William Harper: Self-portraits of the Artist: Sacred & Profane", Franklin Parrasch Gallery, New York, UK (1991); "William Harper: Artist as Alchemist" (touring, 1990–2)

WORKS IN PUBLIC COLLECTIONS The Vatican Museum, Rome, Italy; Victoria & Albert, London, UK; Metropolitan Museum of Art, New York, USA; Schmuckmuseum, Pforzheim, Germany; Museum of Fine Arts, Boston, USA

Petra Hartman

Netherlands   1960

STUDIES Academy of Art, Arnhem, Netherlands

RECENT EXHIBITIONS Galerie Ra, Amsterdam (1988); Gemeente Museum, Arnhem (1990); Kunst Rai, Amsterdam (1992); Glasmuseum, Leerdam (1992–3)

WORKS IN PUBLIC COLLECTIONS Stedelyk Museum, Amsterdam; Centraal Museum, Utrecht; Costume Museum, The Hague, Netherlands; Museum 't Kruithmus, Den Bosch; Gemeente Museum, Arnhem

Anna Heindl

Austria   1950

Lecturer

STUDIES Hochschule für Angewandte Kunst, Vienna, Austria

RECENT EXHIBITIONS Landesmuseum, Graz, Austria (1986); Galerie Farel, Aigle, Switzerland (1991); Galerie Louise Smit, Amsterdam, Netherlands (1991); Galerie V & V, Vienna, Austria (1992)

WORKS IN PUBLIC COLLECTIONS Museum für Angewandte Kunst, Vienna, Austria; Schmuckmuseum, Pforzheim, Germany; Museum Hertogenbosch, Netherlands; Art Gallery of Western Australia, Perth; Collection of the Hochschule für Angewandte Kunst, Vienna, Austria

Therese Hilbert

Germany   1948

STUDIES Kunstgewerbeschule, Zürich, Switzerland; Akademie der Bildenden Künste, Munich, Germany

RECENT EXHIBITIONS "Neoteric Jewellery" (touring through USA, 1992); Schmuckforum, Zürich, Switzerland (1992); Galerie Slavik, Vienna, Austria (1992); "Schmuck: Die Sammlung der Danner Stiftung", Munich, Germany (1993); "Münchner Goldschmiede", Stadtmuseum, Munich, Germany (1993)

WORKS IN PUBLIC COLLECTIONS The Farago Foundation, USA; Schweizerische Edgenossenschaft, Bern, Switzerland; Knapp Collection, New York, USA; Power House Museum, Sydney, Australia; Stedelijk Museum, Amsterdam, Netherlands

Yasuki Hiramatsu

Japan   1926

Professor, Tokyo National University of Fine Arts and Music (Faculty of Fine Arts)

STUDIES Tokyo National University of Fine Arts and Music

AWARDS Craft Centre, Japan (1969); New Craft Exhibition, Tokyo (1970)

RECENT EXHIBITIONS "Metal Ribbon", Atagoyama Gallery, Tokyo, Japan (1989); Electrum Gallery, London (1990); Gallery IF, Tokyo, Japan (1991); "13 Goldschmiede von Amsterdam via Tokyo", Bayerische Akademie der Schönen Künste, Munich, Germany (1993); Facet I, Kunsthal, Rotterdam, Netherlands (1993)

WORKS IN PUBLIC COLLECTIONS Schmuckmuseum, Pforzheim, Germany; Royal College of Art, London, UK; Imperial Household Agency, Japan

Wahei Ikezawa

Japan   1946

Director, Japan Crafts Designers Association; Vice-chair, Japan Jewellery Designers Association

STUDIES Kanazawa Art and Crafts University, Japan (1965–9)

RECENT EXHIBITIONS Galerie No, Lausanne, Switzerland (1991); Gallery Tekona, Nagoya, Japan (1989, 1990); Gallery IF, Tokyo, Japan (1991); Jewelerswerk Galerie, Washington DC, USA (1991)

WORKS IN PUBLIC COLLECTIONS Schmuckmuseum, Pforzheim, Germany

Kazuhiro Itoh

Japan 1948

STUDIES Tama Art University, Tokyo, Japan (1968–71)

RECENT EXHIBITIONS Gallery IF, Tokyo, Japan (1991); Jewelerswerk Galerie, Washington DC, USA (1991); "Maborogi", Kita Kamakura Museum (1992); "Contemporary Japanese Jewellery", Electrum Gallery, London, UK; (1992); "Shiyoku no Utsuwa", Gallery Isogaya, Tokyo (1993)

WORKS IN PUBLIC COLLECTIONS National Museum of Modern Art, Tokyo, Japan; Schmuckmuseum, Pforzheim, Germany; Royal Scottish Museum, Edinburgh, UK

Gilles Jonemann

France 1944

Sculptor and jeweller

STUDIES Beaux-Arts d'Aix-en-Provence, France; Ecole des Arts Appliqués, Paris, France

AWARDS Grand Prix Régional des Métiers d'Arts (1979); Oscar de la Bijouterie Or (1980)

RECENT EXHIBITIONS Sternthaler Galerie, Bonn, Germany (1989); JJDA 25th Anniversary, Tokyo, Japan (1989); Schmuckforum Galerie, Zürich, Switzerland (1990); Contempo'Art Galerie, Nice, France (1990); 3rd Triennale du Bijou, Musée des Arts Décoratifs, Paris, France (1992)

Hermann Jünger

Germany 1928

STUDIES Zeichenakademie, Hanau, Germany; Akademie der Bildenden Künste, Munich, Germnay

RECENT EXHIBITIONS Galerie am Graben, Vienna, Austria (1981); Germanisches Nationalmuseum, Nuremberg, Germany (1988); Museum für Kunsthandwerk, Frankfurt, Germany (1988); Schmuckmuseum, Pforzheim, Germany (1989)

WORKS IN PUBLIC COLLECTIONS Schmuckmuseum, Pforzheim, Germany; Museum für Kunst und Gewerbe, Hamburg, Germany; Museum für Kunsthandwerk, Frankfurt, Germany; Victoria & Albert Museum, London, UK; Art Gallery of Western Australia, Perth, Australia

Svatopluk Kasalý

Czech Republic 1944

Jeweller and glass sculptor

RECENT EXHIBITIONS Galerie Huize de Jonge Jacob, Leuven, Belgium (1986); Galerie M.A. Bazovského, Trenčín, Slovakia (1987); Moravian Gallery, Brno, Czech Republic (1987); Ornamenta 1, Pforzheim, Germany (1989); Špálova Gallery, Prague, Czech Republic (1990)

WORKS IN PUBLIC COLLECTIONS Moravian Gallery, Brno, Czech Republic; Museum of Art and Industry, Prague, Czech Republic; Karin Webster Gallery, Seattle, USA; Gallery Philip Debray, Riihimäki, Finland; Schmuckmuseum, Pforzheim, Germany

Daniel Kruger

Germany 1951

STUDIES University of Stellenbosch, South Africa (1971–2); Michaelis School of Art, Cape Town, South Africa (1973–4); Akademie der Bildenden Künste, Munich, Germany (1974–80)

RECENT EXHIBITIONS "Cross Currents", Australia (1984); Rezac Gallery, Chicago, USA (1989); "Contemporary Jewellery from the Federal Republic of Germany" (touring, 1989); 3rd Triennale du Bijou, Musée des Arts Décoratifs, Paris, France (1992)

WORKS IN PUBLIC COLLECTIONS Gemeente Museum, 'sHertogenbosch, Netherlands; Schmuckmuseum, Pforzheim, Germany; Institut für Auslandsbeziehungen, Stuttgart, Germany

Winfried Krüger

Germany   1944

Freelance designer; Lecturer, Berufskolleg für Formgebung
Schmuck und Gerät, Pforzheim, Germany

STUDIES Goldschmiedeschule, Pforzheim, Germany (1960–2);
Kunst und Werkschule, Pforzheim, Germany (1963–9)

RECENT EXHIBITIONS "Contemporary Jewellery", Barcelona,
Spain (1987); Ornamenta 1, Pforzheim, Germany (1989);
"Beauty is a Story", 'sHertogenbosch, Netherlands (1990);
Galerie Marzee, Nimwegen, Netherlands (1991); Galerie am
Steinweg, Passau, Germany (1992); Galerie Spektrum, Munich,
Germany (1993)

WORKS IN PUBLIC COLLECTIONS Schmuckmuseum, Pforzheim,
Germany; Museum für Kunsthandwerk, Helsinki, Finland;
Museum für Kunst und Gewerbe, Hamburg, Germany; Museum
voor Hedendaagse Kunst, 'sHertogenbosch, Netherlands

Stanley Lechtzin

USA   1936

Professor of Crafts, Tyler School of Art, Temple University,
Philadelphia, USA

STUDIES Wayne State University, Detroit USA; Cranbrook
Academy of Art, Bloomfield Hills, USA

RECENT EXHIBITIONS Museum of Contemporary Crafts, New
York, USA; Carnegie Institute of Technology, Pittsburgh, USA;
University of California, Berkeley, USA; Goldsmith's Hall,
London, UK; Tyler School of Art, Temple University; Philadelphia,
USA

WORKS IN PUBLIC COLLECTIONS American Craft Museum, New
York, USA; University of Fine Arts and Music, Tokyo, Japan;
National Museum of American Art, Renwick Gallery, New
Haven, USA; Goldsmith's Hall, London, UK

Otto Künzli

Germany   1948

Professor, Akademie der Bildenden Künste, Munich, Germany
(Department of Jewellery)

STUDIES Schule für Gestaltung, Zürich, Switzerland (1956–70);
Akademie der Bildenden Künste, Munich, Germany (1972–8)

RECENT EXHIBITIONS Galerie Wittenbrink, Munich, Germany
(1991); "Das dritte Auge", Museum Bellerive, Zürich,
Switzerland (1992); "Oh, Say!", Ezra and Cecile Zilkha Gallery,
Middletown, Connecticut, USA (1992); "The Third Eye",
Kelvingrove Art Gallery and Museum, Glasgow, UK (1992);
"Good Morning, America", Galerie Wittenbrink, Munich,
Germany (1993)

WORKS IN PUBLIC COLLECTIONS Canberra Institute of the Arts,
Canberra, Australia; National Museum of Modern Art, Kyoto,
Japan; Cleveland County Museum, Middlesbrough, UK; Art
Institute, Detroit, USA; Stedelijk Museum, Amsterdam,
Netherlands

Mary Lee Hu

USA   1943

Professor, University of Washington, USA

STUDIES Cranbrook Academy of Art, Bloomfield Hill, USA;
Southern Illinois University, USA

RECENT EXHIBITIONS "The Eloquent Object", Philbrook
Museum, Tulsa, USA (also touring, 1987–9); Concepts Gallery,
Carmel, California, USA (1988); Merrin Gallery, New York, USA
(1989); "Craft Today USA" (touring in Europe, 1989–93);
"Documents Northwest: Northwest Jewellers", Seattle Art
Museum, Seattle, USA (1993)

WORKS IN PUBLIC COLLECTIONS American Craft Museum, New
York, USA; Art Institute of Chicago, USA; Columbus Museum of
Art, Ohio, USA: National Museum of American Art, Renwick
Gallery, New Haven, USA; Victoria & Albert Museum,
London, UK

Jens-Rüdiger Lorenzen

Germany   1942

Professor, Fachhochscule für Gestaltung, Pforzheim, Germany

STUDIES Kunst und Werkschule, Pforzheim, Germany (1965–8)

AWARDS Internationalen Uhrenwettbewerb, Pforzheim (1966);
Bayerischer Staatspreis, Munich (1973)

RECENT EXHIBITIONS Karl-Ernst-Osthause-Museum, Hagen,
Germany; Schmuckmuseum, Pforzheim, Germany;
Landesmuseum, Oldenburg, Germany; Museum für Kunst und
Gewerbe, Hamburg, Germany; Kunsthalle, Nuremberg,
Germany

WORKS IN PUBLIC COLLECTIONS Schmuckmuseum, Pforzheim,
Germany; Victoria & Albert Museum, London, UK; Deutsches
Goldschmiedehaus, Hanau, Germany; Museum für Angewandte
Kunst, Vienna, Austria; Institut für Auslandsbeziehungen,
Stuttgart, Germany

Fritz Maierhofer

Austria   1941

STUDIES Vienna, London

RECENT EXHIBITIONS Victoria & Albert Museum, London, UK
(1988); "Austrian Designs and Architecture", Art Institute,
Chicago, USA (1991); "European Metal", Power House
Museum, Sydney, Australia (1990); Künstlerhaus, Vienna,
Austria (1992); "New Jewels", Kunstgalerie, Knokke,
Belgium (193)

WORKS IN PUBLIC COLLECTIONS Art Gallery of Western
Australia, Perth, Australia; Victoria & Albert Museum, London,
UK; Schmuckmuseum, Pforzheim, Germany; Museum für
Angewandte Kunst, Vienna, Austria; National Museum of
Scotland, Edinburgh, UK

Carlier Makigawa

Australia   1952

Lecturer, Royal Melbourne Institute of Technology, Australia

STUDIES Royal Melbourne Institute of Technology, Australia
(1985–89) Master of Arts

RECENT EXHIBITIONS Jewellery re-designed, British Crafts
Council, England (1982); Contemporary Jewellery, Kyoto
Museum of Modern Art, Japan (1984); Cross Currents, Power
House Museum, Sydney, Australia (1984); 10 Years RA, Galleria
RA Amsterdam, Holland (1986); Ornamenta 1, Schmuck
Museum, Pforzheim, Germany (1989)

WORKS IN PUBLIC COLLECTIONS Australian National Gallery,
Australia; National Gallery of Victoria, Australia; Western
Australia Art Gallery; Power House Museum, Sydney, Australia;
Kyoto Museum of Modern Art

Bruno Martinazzi

Italy   1923

Professor, Academy of Fine Arts, Turin, Italy

STUDIES Turin University, Italy; Art Schools, Turin, Florence and
Rome (1955–6)

RECENT EXHIBITIONS "Contro le Guerre", Museo Diocesano,
Venezia, Italy (1985); Ornamenta 1, Pforzheim, Germany (1989);
Helen Williams Drutt, New York (1990); Studio Ton Berends, The
Hague, Netherlands (1990); Centrum Beeldende Kuns,
Groningen, Netherlands (1992)

WORKS IN PUBLIC COLLECTIONS Galleria d'Arte Moderna,
Museo Civico, Turin, Italy; Schmuckmuseum, Pforzheim,
Germany; 20th-century Museum, Vienna, Austria; Danner
Stiftung, Munich, Germany; Inge Asenbaum Collection, Vienna,
Austria

Wilhelm T. Mattar

Germany 1946

Lecturer, Fachhochscule Schwäbisch Gmünd, Germany

STUDIES Cologne University, Germany (1969–74);
Fachhochschule für Gestaltung, Pforzheim, Germany (1974–9)

RECENT EXHIBITIONS Ornamenta 1, Pforzheim, Germany (1989);
Angemuseum, Erfurt, Germany (1990); "Les Capitales
Européenes du Nouveau Design", Centre Pompidou, Paris,
France (1991); Museum für Kunsthandwerk, Frankfurt, Germany
(1991); Deutsches Klingenmusem, Solingen, Germany (1992)

WORKS IN PUBLIC COLLECTIONS Museum, Cologne, Germany;
Kunstegewerbemuseum, Berlin, Germany; Schmuckmuseum,
Pforzheim, Germany; Kunstindustriemuseum, Copenhagen,
Denmark; Institut für Auslandsbeziehungen, Stuttgart, Germany

Bruce Metcalf

USA 1949

STUDIES Syracuse University, New York, USA; Tyler School of Art,
Philadelphia, USA

RECENT EXHIBITIONS "American Dream, American Extremes",
Museum het Kruithuis, sHertogenbosch, Netherlands; United
States Information Service, Seoul, South Korea (1990);
Jewelerswerk Galerie, Washington DC, USA (1985, 1992); Susan
Cummins Gallery, Mill Valley, California, USA (1990, 1992);
Contacto Directo Galeria, Lisbon, Portugal (1992)

WORKS IN PUBLIC COLLECTIONS Philadelphia Museum of Art,
USA; American Craft Museum, New York, USA; Musée des Arts
Décoratifs, Montreal, Canada; Cranbrook Academy of Art,
Bloomfield Hill, USA

Manfred Nisslmüller

Austria 1940

AWARDS Diamond International Award (1969); Austrian
Würdigungspreis (1992)

RECENT EXHIBITIONS Galerie Louise Smit, Amsterdam,
Netherlands (1989); Galerie Glück, Stuttgart, Germany (1991);
"Configura", Erfurt, Germany (1991); "Eines und Anderes",
Werkstadt, Graz, Austria (1993); Facet 1, Kunsthal, Rotterdam,
Netherlands (1993)

FWORKS IN PUBLIC COLLECTIONS Schmuck-Stücke, Munich,
Germany; Zeichen am Körper, Linz, Austria; Aluminium,
Cologne, Germany

Johannes Oppermann

Germany 1960

STUDIES Fachhochscule für Gestaltung, Schwäbisch Gmünd,
Germany

RECENT EXHIBITIONS Galerie Marzee, Nijmegen, Netherlands
(1989); Galerie Hipotesi, Barcelona, Spain (1990); "Les Capitales
Européennes du Nouveau Design", Centre Pompidou, Paris,
France (1991); "Arsenale", Klingenmuseum, Solingen, Germany
(1992); "The Magic of the Ring", Electrum Gallery, London, UK
(1993)

WORKS IN PUBLIC COLLECTIONS Kunstindustriemuseum,
Copenhagen, Denmark; Kunstindustriemuseum, Trondheim,
Norway; Städtisches Museum, Schwäbisch Gmünd, Germany;
Museum für Kunst und Gewerbe, Hamburg, Germany

Barbara Paganin

Italy 1961

STUDIES Istituto Statale d'Arte, Venezia, Italy; Accademia di Belle
Arti, Venezia, Italy

AWARDS "Schmuck '87", Hause der Kunst, Monaco (1987);
Design Wettburg Cointreau, Monaco (1990)

RECENT EXHIBITIONS Kammen, Museum Boymans van
Beuningen, Rotterdam, Netherlands (1989); "Aura", Galleria
olella Fondazione Bevilacoqua La Masa, Venezia, Italy (1990);
Biennale dei Giovani Artisti dell'Europa Mediterranea, Marseilles,
France (1990); 3rd Triennale du Bijou, Musée des Arts Décoratifs,
Paris, France (1992); Facet I, Kunsthal, Rotterdam,
Netherlands (1993)

WORKS IN PUBLIC COLLECTIONS Musei d'Arte Moderna
ca'Pesaro, Venezia, Italy; Museum Boymans van Beuningen,
Rotterdam, Netherlands

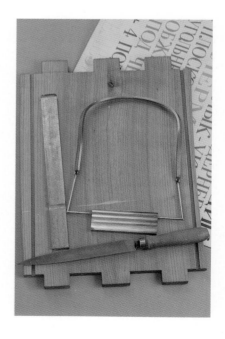

Francesco Pavan

Italy 1937

STUDIES Istituto d'Arte Pietro Selvatico, Padua, Italy

RECENT EXHIBITIONS Galerie Louise Smit, Amsterdam, Netherlands (1988); Helen Williams Drutt, New York, USA (1988); Galerie für Modernen Schmuck, Frankfurt, Germany (1991); Galerie Wassermann, Munich, Germany (1992); "13 Goldschmiede von Amsterdam via Tokyo", Bayerische Akademie der Schönen Künste, Munich, Germany (1993)

WORKS IN PUBLIC COLLECTIONS Schmuckmuseum, Pforzheim, Germany; Danner Stiftung, Munich, Germany; Helen Williams Drutt, Philadelphia, USA

Ruudt Peters

Netherlands 1950

Lecturer, Gerrit Rietveld Academie, Amsterdam, Netherlands (Jewellery Department)

STUDIES Gerrit Rietveld Academie, Amsterdam, Netherlands (1970–4)

RECENT EXHIBITIONS Galerie V & V, Vienna Austria (1991); Van Reekum Museum, Apeldoorn, Netherlands (1991); Galerie Spektrum, Munich, Germany (1992); De Krabbedans, Eindhoven, Netherlands (1992); Galerie Marzee, Nijmegen, Netherlands (1992)

WORKS IN PUBLIC COLLECTIONS Schmuckmuseum, Pforzheim, Germany; Museum für Angewandte Kunst, Hamburg, Germany; Stedelijk Museum, Amsterdam, Netherlands; Museum of Modern Art, New York, USA; Museum für Angewandte Kunst, Vienna, Austria

Mario Pinton

Italy 1919

STUDIES Scuola d'Arte, Padua, Italy; Istituto d'Arte, Venezia, Italy

RECENT EXHIBITIONS "Ring Throughout", Paris, France (1982); Triennale, Tokyo, Japan (1986); "Orafi Padovani" (touring in Germany, Italy, Switzerland, USA, Canada, 1984, 1986–7); Galerie Cada, Munich, Germany (1986); "New Jewels", Kunstgalerie, Knokke, Belgium (1991)

WORKS IN PUBLIC COLLECTIONS Schmuckmuseum, Pforzheim, Germany; Victoria & Albert Museum, London, UK; Museum für Kunst und Gewerbe, Hamburg, Germany; Musée des Arts Décoratifs, Paris, France

Ramón Puig Cuyás

Spain 1953

Lecturer, Escola Massana, Barcelona, Spain

STUDIES Escola Massana, Barcelona (1969–74); University of Barcelona (Faculty of Fine Arts), Spain (1980–2)

RECENT EXHIBITIONS GU Galerie, Barcelona (1989); Contacto Directo Galeria, Lisbon, Portugal (1989); Helen Williams Drutt, New York, USA (1990); Hilde Leis Galerie, Hamburg, Germany (1990); "Les Soirs d'Été", Galerie Jocelyne Gobeil, Montreal, Canada (1993)

WORKS IN PUBLIC COLLECTIONS Schmuckmuseum, Pforzheim, Germany; Kunstindustriemuseum, Copenhagen, Denmark; Danner Stiftung, Munich, Germany; Museum of Art, Montreal, Canada

Wolfgang Rahs

Austria 1952

STUDIES Fachschule für Gestaltendes Metalhandwerk, Graz, Austria

RECENT EXHIBITIONS "Mauspfad", Forum für Schmuck und Design, Cologne, Germany (1987); Ornamenta 1, Pforzheim, Germany (1989); "Jewellery: Means: Meaning", Ewing Gallery, Tennessee, USA (touring, 1989), "Feilübung", Werkstadt, Graz, Austria (1990)

WORKS IN PUBLIC COLLECTIONS Ministry of Education and Arts, Vienna, Austria; Landesmuseum Joanneum, Graz, Austria

Wendy Ramshaw

UK   1939

STUDIES College of Art and Industrial Design, Newcastle-upon-Tyne, 1957–60; University of Reading, 1960–61

AWARDS Council of Industrial Design Award, 1972; Art in Architecture Award, Royal Society of Arts, 1993

RECENT EXHIBITIONS Goldsmiths' Hall, London (1973); "Wendy Ramshaw", Victoria & Albert Museum, London (1982); "Wendy Ramshaw – David Watkins", Schmuckmuseum, Pforzheim, Germany (1987); "Picasso's Ladies", Birmingham City Art Gallery, England (1990); "From Paper to Gold", Royal Festival Hall, London (1990)

WORKS IN PUBLIC COLLECTIONS Victoria & Albert Museum, London, England; Philadelphia Museum of Art, USA; Stedelijk Museum, Amsterdam, Netherlands; The Museum of Modern Art, Kyoto, Japan; Musée des Arts Decoratifs, Paris, France

Gerd Rothmann

Germany   1941

STUDIES Staatlichen Zeichenakademie, Hanau, Germany

RECENT EXHIBITIONS Galerie Spektrum, Munich, Germany (1989); Rezac Gallery, Chicago, USA (1989); Galerie Fred Jan, Munich, Germany (1990); "Europäisches Kunsthandwerk 1991", Stuttgart, Germany (1991); Society for Contemporary Crafts, Pittsburgh, USA (1992)

WORKS IN PUBLIC COLLECTIONS Stedelijk Museum, Amsterdam, Netherlands; Victoria & Albert Museum, London, UK; Museum of Modern Art, New York, USA; Stadtmuseum, Munich, Germany; Danner Stiftung, Munich, Germany

Philip Sajet

Netherlands   1953

STUDIES Gerrit Rietveld Academie, Amsterdam, Netherlands

RECENT EXHIBITIONS Ornamenta 1, Pforzheim, Germany (1989); Galerie Marzee, Nijmegen, Netherlands (1990); "Neoteric Jewellery" (touring through USA, 1992); "Arsenale", Klingenmuseum, Solingen, Germany (1992); Gallery Carin Delcourt van Krimpen, Rotterdam, Netherlands (1991–3)

WORKS IN PUBLIC COLLECTIONS Stedelijk Museum, Amsterdam, Netherlands; Museum het Kruithuis, 'sHertogenbosch, Netherlands; Van Reekum Museum, Apeldoorn, Netherlands; Gemeente Museum, Arnhem, Netherlands

Marjorie Schick

USA   1941

Professor of Art, Pittsburg State University, Kansas, USA

STUDIES University of Wisconsin, Madison, USA; Indiana University, Bloomington, USA; Sir John Cass School of Art, London, UK

RECENT EXHIBITIONS Museum of Applied Art, Trondheim, Norway (1989); Retrospective, School of Fine Arts, Indiana University, USA (1990); "Body Art", Security Pacific Gallery, Costa Mesa, California, USA (1990); Galerie Ra, Amsterdam, Netherlands (1991); "Design Visions", 2nd International Crafts Triennale, Art Gallery of Western Australia, Perth, Australia (1992)

WORKS IN PUBLIC COLLECTIONS National Museum of Contemporary Art, Seoul, South Korea; Museum of Applied Art, Trondheim, Norway; National Museum of Modern Art, Kyoto, Japan; Cleveland Country Museum, Middlesbrough, UK; Museum of Applied Art, Oslo, Norway

Bernhard Schobinger

Switzerland 1946

Freeland jeweller

STUDIES Allgemeine Klasse Kunstgewerbeschule, Germany (1962–7)

AWARDS International Diamonds Award, New York, USA (1971); Deutscher Schmuck und Edelsteinpreis (1972)

RECENT EXHIBITIONS Museum Schloss Morsbroich, Leverkusn, Germany (1986); Galerie Ziegler, Zürich, Switzerland (1990); Museum für Kunsthandwerk, Frankfurt, Germany (1990); Grassimuseum, Leipzig, Germany (1001); Facet I, Kunsthal, Rotterdam, Netherlands (1993)

WORKS IN PUBLIC COLLECTIONS Landesmuseum, Stuttgart, Germany; Stedelijk Museum, Amsterdam, Netherlands; Museum des Kunsthandwerks, Grassimuseum, Leipzig, Germany; Sammlung Voegele, Switzerland; Kunstsammlung der Schweizerischen Eidgenossenschaft, Switzerland

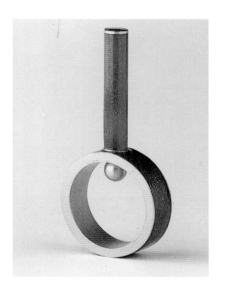

Deganit Schocken

Israel 1947

Lecturer, North Bloomfield College of Art and Design, Haifa, Israel

STUDIES Bezalel Academy of Art and Design, Jerusalem, Israel (1968–73); Sir John Cass School of Art, London, UK; Hornsey School of Art, London, UK

RECENT EXHIBITIONS Helen Williams Drutt, New York, USA (1989); "Using Gold and Silver", Schwäbisch Gmünd, Germany (1990); Electrum Gallery, London, UK (1991); Bertha Urdang Gallery, New York, USA (1991); 3rd Triennale du Bijou, Musée des Arts Décoratifs, Paris, France (1992)

WORKS IN PUBLIC COLLECTIONS Israel Museum, Jerusalem, Israel; Brooklyn Museum, New York, USA; Helen Williams Drutt, USA

Robert Smit

Netherlands 1971

STUDIES Technische School, Delft, Netherlands (1954–7); Staatliche Kunst und Werkschule, Pforzheim, Germany (1963–6)

AWARDS Bayerischen Staatspreis, Munich, Germany (1967)

RECENT EXHIBITIONS Galerie Louise Smit, Amsterdam, Netherlands (1989, 1992); Helen Williams Drutt, New York, USA (1990); Studio Ton Brends, The Hague, Netherlands (1991); Galerie Spektrum, Munich, Germany (1992); 3rd Triennale du Bijou, Musée des Arts Décoratifs, Paris, France (1992)

WORKS IN PUBLIC COLLECTIONS Stedelijk Museum, Amsterdam, Netherlands: Schmuckmuseum, Pforzheim, Germany; Centraal Museum. Utrecht, Netherlands; Danner Stiftung, Munich, Germany; Gemeente Museum, The Hague, Netherlands

Rachelle Thiewes

USA 1952

Professor of Art, University of Texas, El Paso, USA

STUDIES Southern Illinois University, Carbondale, USA; Kent State University, Ohio, USA

AWARDS "Gold '82", International Gold Competition, New York (1982)

RECENT EXHIBITIONS CDK Gallery, New York, US (1989); Jewelerswerk Galerie, Washington DC, USA (1989); Dartmouth College, New Hampshire, USA (1991); Galveston Art Centre, Texas, USA (1993); El Paso Museum of Art, Texas, USA (1993)

WORKS IN PUBLIC COLLECTIONS Arkansas Art Centre, Arkansas, USA; Art Institute, Chicago, USA; University of Texas, El Paso, USA; Art Museum, Evansville, Indiana, USA; American Craft Museum, New York, USA

Detlef Thomas

Germany   1959

STUDIES Akademie der Bildenden Künste, Munich, Germany
(1983–8)

RECENT EXHIBITIONS Galerie für Modernen Schmuck, Frankfurt,
Germany (1990); Rezac Gallery, Chicago, USA (1990); Galerie
Louise Smit, Amsterdam, Netherlands (1990, 1992); Contacto
Directo Galeria, Lisbon, Portugal (1992)

WORKS IN PUBLIC COLLECTIONS Danner Stiftung, Munich,
Germany; Royal College of Art, London, UK; Museum voor
Hedendaagse Kunst, 'sHertogenbosch, Netherlands;
Schmuckmuseum, Pforzheim, Germany; Musée des Arts
Décoratifs, Paris, France

Andreas Treykorn

Germany   1960

RECENT EXHIBITIONS Galerie Marzee, Nijmegen, Netherlands
(1988); Galerie am Graben, Vienna, Austria (1988); Galerie
Spektrum, Munich, Germany (1989); "Europäisches
Kunsthandwerk 1991", Stuttgart, Germany (1991); 3rd Triennale
du Bijou, Musée des Arts Décoratifs, Paris, France (1992)

WORKS IN PUBLIC COLLECTIONS Danner Stiftung, Munich,
Germany; Österreichisches Museum für Angewandte Kunst,
Vienna, Austria

Tone Vigeland

Norway   1938

STUDIES National College of Art, Craft and Design, Oslo, Norway
(1955–7); Technical College for Jewellers, Oslo (1957)

AWARDS Jacob Prize (1965); City of Oslo Arts Prize (1987); Prins
Eugen Medal (1988)

RECENT EXHIBITIONS Kunstindustrimuseet, Oslo, Norway
(1986); Artwear, New York, USA (1987); Kunstnerforbundet,
Oslo, Norway (1989, 1993); Electrum Gallery, London, UK
(1990); 3rd Triennale du Bijou, Musée des Arts Décoratifs, Paris,
France (1992)

WORKS IN PUBLIC COLLECTIONS Museum of Modern Art, New
York, USA; Cooper Hewitt Museum, New York, USA;
Smithsonian Institution, Washington DC, USA; Victoria & Albert
Museum, London, UK; National Museum of Modern Art,
Tokyo, Japan

Graziano Visintin

Italy   1954

Lecturer, Istituto d'Arte Pietro Selvatico, Padua, Italy

STUDIES Istituto d'Arte Pietro Selvatico, Padua, Italy

RECENT EXHIBITIONS Galerie Marzee, Nijmegen, Netherlands;
Galerie Louise Smit, Amsterdam, Netherlands; Galerie Treykorn,
Berlin, Germany; "Rarefrazioni", Galleria Civica, Portugal;
Galerie Wassermann, Munich, Germany

WORKS IN PUBLIC COLLECTIONS Schmuckmuseum, Pforzheim,
Germany; Danner Stiftung, Munich, Germany

David Watkins

UK   1940

STUDIES University of Reading, Fine Art, 1959–63

AWARDS Crafts Advisory Committee, Bursary

RECENT EXHIBITIONS "David Watkins: Jewellery", Stedelijk Museum, Amsterdam (1986). "Wendy Ramshaw – David Watkins", Schmuckmuseum, Pforzheim, Germany (1987); Contemporary Applied Arts, London (1989); Helen Williams Drutt, New York, USA (1989); "Jewellery Biennial: Facet I", Kunsthal, Rotterdam (1993)

WORKS IN PUBLIC COLLECTIONS Australian National Gallery, Canberra; National Museum of Modern Art, Tokyo, Japan; Schmuckmuseum, Pforzheim, Germany; Stedilijk Museum, Amsterdam, Netherlands; Victoria & Albert Museum, London, UK

Anette Wohlleber

Germany   1962

STUDIES Fachhochscule für Gestaltung, Profzheim, Germany (1982–6); Nova Scotia College of Art and Design, Halifax, Canada (1986)

AWARDS Kunsthandwerker, Landesausstellung-Württemberg (1992)

RECENT EXHIBITIONS Werkstattgalerie, Berlin, Germany (1990); Galerie Michèle Zeller, Bern, Switzerland (1990, 1991); Schmuckforum, Zürich, Switzerland (1991); Galerie Marzee, Nijmegen, Netherlands (1991); Galerie Hilde Leiss, Hamburg, Germany (1992)

WORKS IN PUBLIC COLLECTIONS Schmuckmuseum, Pforzheim, Germany

Irmgard Zeitler

Germany   1957

STUDIES Fachschule für Glas und Schmuck, Kaufbeuren, Germany (1977–80); Akademie der Bildenden Künste, Munich, Germany (1980–6)

RECENT EXHIBITIONS Galerie für Modernen Schmuck, Frankfurt, Germany (1988); "10 Goldsmiths", Rezac Gallery, Chicago, USA (1988); Galerie Treykorn, Berlin, Germany (1991); 4-Raumdaxer, Munich, Germany (1992); "Münchner Goldschmiede", Stadtmuseum, Munich, Germany (1993)

Othmar Zschaler

Switzerland   1930

RECENT EXHIBITIONS Galerie Maya Behn, Zürich, Switzerland (1982); Galerie Atrium, Basle, Switzerland (1983)

WORKS IN PUBLIC COLLECTIONS Hessisches Landesmuseum, Darmstadt, Germany; Schmuckmuseum, Pforzheim, Germany; Landesmuseum, Zürich, Switzerland; Historisches Museum, Bern, Switzerland; Sammlung des Kanton Bern, Bern, Switzerland

Index of Artists and Projects

B

Babetto, Giampaolo
  Inspiration for a necklace   10
  Brooch 1992   28
  Neckpiece 1992   29
  Bracelet 1991   30
  Brooch 1992   31
Bahrs, Ulrike
  4 levels reflect into the sun, neckpiece
    1991   32
  Egg, Wool and Metal Necklace and
    bracelet 1990   33
  Egg, Wool and Metal 1990   196, 197
Bakker, Gijs
  Adam Collar 1988   34
  Nesty Brooch 1991   35
  Face Brooch 1991   35
  Nipple 1991   191
  The Tongue 1989   191
Bennet, James
  Rocaille #5 Brooch 1992   36
  Petrosa #4 Brooch 1992   37
  Petrosa #1 Brooch 1991   38
  Rocaille #11 Brooch 1992   39
Blåvarp, Liz
  Neckpiece 1990   40
  Detail of neckpiece 1993   40
  Neckpiece 1992   40
Boekhoudt, Onno
  Models for rings in painted wood   15
  8 rings 1989   42
  Brooch 1993   42
  Ring 1990   45
  Brooch 1991   45
  Brooch 1993   45
Bott, Rudolf
  Rings 1991   46
  Pins/Brooches 1992   46
  Necklace 1989   47
  Necklace 1989   47

C

Capdevila, Joaquim
  Pin 1993   48
  Mediterraneo Brooch 1993   49
Cepka, Anton
  Sketches for Brooches 1993   12
  Brooch 1990   50
  Brooch 1989   51
  Brooch 1990   51
Chang, Peter
  Bracelets 1987   199
  Brooch 1992   52
  Bracelet 1993   53
Cohn, Susan
  Models for the series . . . *and does it work?*
    1990   24
  Models for the series . . . *Cosmetic
    Manipulations* 1992   24
  Cosmetic Manipulations – Chin Earring and
    correction piece 1992   54
  Cosmetic Manipulations – Nose Brooch
    (and nose correction piece) 1992   54
  Cosmetic Manipulations – Chin Earrings
    1992   54
  Microphone Brooch 1990   55
  Cosmetic Manipulations – Chin 1992   198
  Cosmetic Manipulations – Nose 1992   198

Cousens, Cynthia
  Rings 1992   56
  Rings 1992   57
  Cocoon and Whisper rings 1993   57

D

de Wolf, Lam
  Work in progress on the neckpiece *Kubus*
    (also part of a wall hanging) 1990   17
Dobler, Georg
  Brooch 1990   58
  Brooch 1991   58
  Brooch 1989   59
  Brooch 1990   59
Domenech, Xavier
  Matagi Brooch 1992   61
  Nook Brooch 1993   61
  Soma Brooch 1993   61
  Venus Sativa I and Venus Sativa II Brooches
    1993   61
van der Donk, Jacomyn
  Bracelet 1993   62
  Ring 1993   62
  Ring 1993   62
  Ring 1992   63
  Ring 1993   63
  Ring #3A   189
  Ring #1A   189
  Ring #4A   189

F

Fisch, Arline M
  Black and White Plaid #1   65
Flöckinger, Gerda
  Ear pieces 1993   67

G

Gralnick, Lisa
  Bracelet 1987   68
  Brooch 1988   68
  Brooch 1987   69
  Bracelet 1987   204

H

Harper, William
  Drawing/collage: *Self-portrait of the Artist
    . . . Possessed* 1992   16
  Ripe Blossom II Brooch   70
  *Grotesque self-portrait of the Artist as the
    Goddess Kali* Brooch   70
  Self-portrait of the Artist as a Haruspex
    Brooch 1990   72
  Faberge's Seed #7 Brooch 1993   72
Hartman, Petra
  Heart with Teardrop 1992   184
  Giant Necklace 1992 200
Heindl, Anna
  Ohr/Ear Brooch 1991   74
  Tuten/Bags Necklace 1992   74
  Earrings 1991   75
  Necklace 1992   75
Hiramatsu, Yasuki
  Bracelet 1992   78
  Necklace 1989   78
  Clown 1991   204

Hilbert, Therese
  Brooch 1991   76
  Brooch 1992   76
  Brooch 1991   77
  Brooch 1992   77
  Brooch 1991   77
  Brooch 1991   77

I

Ikezawa, Wahei
  Regenerat Neckpiece 1991   80
  Regenerat Neckpiece 1991   80
Itoh, Kazuhiro
  Necklace 1992   82
  Necklace 1992   83
  Bracelet, pendant, ring 1991   83

J

Jonemann, Gilles
  Necklace 1990   84
  Brooch 1988   85
Jünger, Hermann
  A page of sketches 1992   23
  Brooch 1992   86
  3 Brooches 1992   87
  2 Pendants 1990   89
  3 Brooches 1992   87

K

Kasaly, Svatopluk
  Necklace 1991   90
  Necklace 1991   91
  Necklace 1991   185
Kruger, Daniel
  Ring 1992   92
  Ring 1993   92
  Ring 1993   92
  Ring 1993   93
Krüger, Winfried
  Abschied von Berlin/Farewell to Berlin
    Brooch 1990–91   94
  Faust Brooch 1990–91   94
  *Wenn ich ein Röslein wär/If I were a small
    rose* Brooch 1990–91   94
Künzli, Otto
  Oh say! Brooch 1991   96
  Black Mickey Mouse Brooch 1991   97
  UFO-Unidentified Found Objects Pendants
    1992   98
  1492 – When Mickey Mouse was Born
    Shoulder piece – 1992   99

L

Lechtzin, Stanley
  CAD Wire frame models for the bracelet
    Archbrace # 38F 1992   19
  SWPTORC. TIFF Neckpiece 1994   100
  PENTSPLC. TIF Bracelet 1992   101
  XRACE TIF Bracelet 1992   101
Lee Hu, Mary
  Choker #80 Neckpiece 1992   102
  Choker #78 Neckpiece 1991   102
  Bracelets #43, 44, 45 1989   103
  Earrings #136 1990   103

Lorenzen, Jens-Rüdiger
  Drawings, text and photographs in
    connection with *Legende No. 9* 1992   11
  Legende No. 9 Brooch 1992   104
  Brooch 1992   105
  Ring 1992   106
  Ring 1992   107

M
Magikawa, Carlier
  Brooch 1991   195
  2 Brooches 1991   112
  Object 1992   112
  Brooch 1991   113
  2 Rings/objects   113
Maierhofer, Fritz
  Models for three brooches 1991   18
  Ring 1991   108
  Brooch 1991   109
  Detail of Brooch   110
  Brooch 1991   111
  Ring #4   188
Martinazzi, Bruno
  Drawing for the ring *Dike* 1992   20
  Epistomy Brooch 1993   114
  Kaos Brooch 1992   115
  Metamorphosis Bracelet 1992   116
  Reversibility Bracelet 1992   117
Mattar, Wilhelm T.
  Model for a brooch   18
  Brooch 1991   118
  Ring 1989   119
  Brooch 1987   119
  Lift Ring 1985   119
Metcalf, Bruce
  Design Lesson #4 Pin 1992   121
  Wood Pin #57 Pin 1990   121
  Wood Pin #69 1991   187

N
Nisslmüller, Manfred
  Fur eine Brosche/For a Brooch   122
  *Fur den schönen Finger/For the beautiful
    finger* Ring 1989/90   123
  Taschenrecorder/Portable stereo Accoustic
    jewellery 1985–93   123

O
Opperman, Johannes
  Ring 1991   124
  Ring 1993   124
  Ring 1991   125
  Ring 1993   125
  Ring 1993   125

P
Paganin, Barbara
  Radiolari Rings 1992   126
  Microftalmo Ring 1993   126
  Pteri Gota Bracelet 1993
Pavan, Francesco
  Vibrazioni cromatiche Brooch 1992   128
  Vibrazioni cromatiche Brooch 1992   129
  Vibrazioni cromatiche Brooch 1992   129
Peters, Ruudt
  Maciavelli Neckpiece 1992   130
  Antinous Neckpiece 1992   131
Pinton, Mario
  Brooch 1986   132
  Brooch 1990   133

Puig Cuyas, Ramón
  La Porta/The Door Brooch 1992   134
  El Llop/The Wolf Brooch 1992   135
  Un Dia Quansevol/An Anyday Day   135

R
Rahs, Wolfgang
  Case on Radwerk/Kiste am Radwerk
    1990   13
  *Case at Graz Main Station/Kiste am
    Hauptbahnhof Graz* 1990   13
  Certomlyk Neckpiece 1990–92   136
  Kelemeskaja Neckpiece 1990–93   136
  Workbench Banquet Shoulder piece
    1993   136
  Workbench Banquet Necklace 1993   136
  Workbench Banquet 1993   193
Ramshaw, Wendy
  Drawing for *Earrings for Woman with
    Large Profile* 1989   22
  Transformer Ring on stand 1992   138
  Rays of the Sun Neckpiece 1989   139
  Transpiration Rings on stands 1992   140
  2 Brooches 1992   140
  Catherine Wheel 1990   200
  Earrings for Woman with Large Profile
    1989   203
Rothmann, Gerd
  Vier-Finger-Armreif/Four finger bracelet
    Bracelet 1992   142
  Von ihm für sie/From him for her Bracelet
    1990   142
  *Wachskugeln flach gedruckt/Wax balls
    pressed flat* Neckpiece 1988   143
  Siefelring/Signet ring Ring 1987   143
  *Wachskugeln flach gedrückt/Wax balls
    pressed flat* 1988   192

S
Sajet, Philip
  Painting (sketch) for the neckpiece
    Thunder and Lightning 1993   21
  Thunder and Lightning Neckpiece
    1993   144
  Byzantine Ring Ring 1988   145
  Flower Ring Ring 1991   145
  Der Chinesische Ring/The Chinese Ring
    Ring 1990   145
Schick, Marjorie
  Collar 1993   146
  Live Show Collar 1992   146
  Wall Sculpture with Armlet Armlet
    1992   147
Schobinger, Bernhard
  *Mit Licht gebohrter Diamant/Diamond
    drilled with light* Ring 1991   148
  Holiday in Cambodia
    Bracelet 1990   149
  Paradiesgarten/Garden of Paradise
    Armband 1990   150
  Flaschenhalskette/Bottle necklace
    Necklace 1990   150
  *Sonia with Rusted Cross/Sonja mit
    Sagenkreuz*   186
  *Sonia with Bottle Neckpiece/Sonja mit
    Flaschenhalskette*   186
Schocken, Deganit
  Signs of Personality Body piece 1990   152

Smit, Robert
  Bello – A Double Portrait Brooch
    1992   154
  Konigin Bello/Queen Bello Brooch
    1992   154
  Pendant 1991   157
  Chain 1991   157

T
Thiewes, Rachelle
  Reflections of St. Mary's Necklace
    1991   158
  Silent Dance Brooch 1992   158
  Reflections of St. Mary's Necklace
    1991   161
  Silent Dance Brooch 1992   161
Thomas, Detlef
  Neckpiece 1990   162
  Ring 1992   163
  Ring 1992   163
  Ring 1992   163
  Ring 1993   163
Treykorn, Andreas
  Brooch 1993   165

V
Vigeland, Tone
  Cap 1992   166
  Cap 1992   166
  Neckpiece 1992   167
  Bracelet 1992   168
  Neckpiece 1992   169
  Neckpiece 1992   169
  Silver Cap 22 1992   202
  Silver Cap 33 1992   202
Visintin, Graziano
  Necklace 1990   170
  Bracelet 1990   171
  Necklace 1992   171

W
Watkins, David
  *Printed screen dumps of CAD Models
    for brooches* 1989   25
  Torus 280 (B2) Neckpiece 1989   172
  Surf 1 Brooch 1990   172
  Torus 280 (B1) Neckpiece 1989   173
  Leaf Pin 1 Brooch 1993   174
  Wheel Pin 2 Brooch 1993   175
  Torus 280 (B3) 1990   207
Wohlleber, Anette
  Windmühle/Windmill Brooch 1991   176
  Hochofen/Blast-furnace Brooch 1991   176
  Nudelwagen/Noodlecar Brooch 1991   177
  Wagen/Car Brooch 1991   177

Z
Zeitler, Irmgard
  Rose Ball Pendant 1992   179
  Berry Pendant 1990   179
  Cactus Flowers Ear piece 1990   179
Zschaler, Othmar
  Bracelet 1992   180
  Brooch 1992   181
  Printed screen dumps of CAD models for
    brooches 1989   25

Photographic Credits